FOLK ROOTS and MYTHIC WINGS
in SARAH ORNE JEWETT
and TONI MORRISON

FOLK ROOTS and MYTHIC WINGS in SARAH ORNE JEWETT and TONI MORRISON

THE CULTURAL FUNCTION OF NARRATIVE

Marilyn Sanders Mobley

LOUISIANA STATE UNIVERSITY PRESS

Baton Rouge and London

Designer: Glynnis Phoebe
Typeface: Bembo
Typesetter: G&S Typesetters, Inc.
Printer and binder: Thomson-Shore, Inc.

Library of Congress Cataloging-in-Publication Data
Mobley, Marilyn Sanders, 1952–
    Folk roots and mythic wings in Sarah Orne Jewett and Toni Morrison :
the cultural function of narrative / Marilyn Sanders Mobley.
        p.   cm.
    Includes bibliographical references and index.
    ISBN 0-8071-1660-2 (cloth)
        1. American fiction—Women authors—History and criticism.
    2. Jewett, Sarah Orne, 1849–1909—Criticism and interpretation.
    3. Morrison, Toni—Criticism and interpretation.   4. Literature and
    anthropology—United States.   5. Women and literature—United
    States.   6. Folklore in literature.   7. Myth in literature.
    I. Title.
    PS374.W6M63   1991   91-15031
    813.009'9287—dc20   CIP

The author is grateful to Toni Morrison for permission to quote from her works. She is also grateful to *Colby Library Quarterly* for permission to use material from her essay "Rituals of Flight and Return: The Ironic Journeys of Sarah Orne Jewett's Female Characters," which appeared in that journal's Volume XXII (March, 1986), 36–42. Some of the material used in Chapter 4 originally appeared in the author's essay "Narrative Dilemma: Jadine as Cultural Orphan in Toni Morrison's *Tar Baby*," *Southern Review*, XXIII (Autumn, 1987), 761–70.

To my mother, Priscilla, who gave me roots;
to my father, Delbert, who gave me wings;
to my husband, Michael, who gave me love; and
to my sons, Rashad and Jamal, who gave me perspective.

CONTENTS

ACKNOWLEDGMENTS

The process of bringing this project to fruition was long and arduous. The topic of this book began as a hunch, evolved into a belief, and became an assertion that I had to make. But even before the hunch came ideas I had unconsciously collected over the years, beginning possibly with my studies at Barnard College, where Professor Quandra Prettyman formally introduced me to the African-American folk tradition in the fiction of Zora Neale Hurston. I later had the honor of studying with author Ralph Ellison for one semester at New York University. Mr. Ellison not only planted the seeds that showed me how to connect folklore and African-American literature but also introduced me to the work of Constance Rourke and thus gave me a critical resource that I returned to in the early stages of this study.

For encouraging me to pursue the connection I saw between Jewett and Morrison and for being so generous with his time and assistance, I must first thank Professor Gary Lee Stonum of the English Department of Case Western Reserve University. I thank Professor Roger Salomon for his wise counsel and careful reading of my first paper on Jewett. I also thank Professor Deborah Ellis for her enthusiastic response to my first paper on Morrison and for the times we discussed the joys and challenges we face as women who have taken on the roles of scholar, wife, and mother.

I would like to acknowledge a host of other people, but for the sake of brevity, I will name only a few and trust that I have at some point expressed my gratitude to those whose names do not appear here. For listening to my ideas and for sharing theirs, I thank Henry Louis Gates, Jr., Norman Harris, Barbara Johns, Willa Lowe, Audrey and John McCluskey, Deborah McDowell, Nellie McKay, Jackie McLendon, James Olney, Quandra Prettyman, Valerie Smith, Ellease Southerland, Claudia Tate, Roberta Wollens, and Linda Williamson-Nelson.

I especially want to thank my editor, Trudie Calvert, and also John Easterly and others at Louisiana State University Press for support and extraordinary patience during the revising and editing of this manuscript. I am deeply grateful for the assistance I received from my two typists, Monica Giordano and Mary Kay Burkart.

For their special friendship, I thank Jacquie McLemore, Glenda Moss, and Betty Roberson. I owe a special thanks to Sheila Abdus-Salaam, my friend who has been the sister I always wanted.

I also owe a special thanks to my Aunt Monica and Uncle Harold, who gave me their love, their encouragement, and a room of my own in their home during the summer of 1986. My time with my aunt was the spiritual retreat I needed to move from preparation to the actual writing of this book. In addition, I thank my mother-in-law, Annie Mobley, for allowing me to convert her upstairs into a combination study, library, and bedroom during the summer of 1984. I especially appreciate the encouragement I received from the rest of my family and friends.

My mother has been a constant source of inspiration. For the times she and my stepfather, Chuck, came to my rescue by helping us with our children, I am forever grateful. I am also thankful for the encouragement I received from my father, Delbert, and my brothers, Calvin, Bennett, and Rowland.

Finally, I thank the three people who have endured the most— my two wonderful sons and my remarkable husband. I commend Rashad and Jamal for patience and understanding far beyond their young ages. My utmost love and gratitude go to my husband, Michael, not only for wanting me to achieve this dream as much as I wanted it, but for giving me the love and support I needed to make it happen.

FOLK ROOTS and MYTHIC WINGS
in SARAH ORNE JEWETT
and TONI MORRISON

INTRODUCTION

THE WOMAN WRITER AS CULTURAL ARCHIVIST AND REDEMPTIVE SCRIBE

> I am always saying . . . Plato's great reminder that the "best thing we can do for the people of a State is to make them acquainted with each other."
> —Sarah Orne Jewett

> We don't live in places where we can hear those stories anymore; parents don't sit around and tell their children those classical, mythological, archetypal stories that we heard years ago.
> —Toni Morrison

At the center of Sarah Orne Jewett's *The Country of the Pointed Firs* is the story of Mrs. Almira Todd, an herbalist and conjure woman. Her expertise with various herbs brings her in contact with village neighbors who come to her, rather than to the village doctor, for physical and spiritual healing. Not only is Mrs. Todd central to the life of her village, but the stories she shares with the narrator acquaint her with the region and transform the narrator's naive perceptions of country people and country life. Described as a "simple-hearted woman" in whom "life was very strong . . . as if some force of nature were personified in her . . . and gave her cousinship to the ancient deities," Mrs. Todd represents the female archetypal hero among Jewett's fictional characters.[1] At the center of Toni Morrison's *Song of Solomon* and of the story of Milkman Dead's quest for identity is the story of Pilate, who as a female sage and conjure woman is Mrs. Todd's African-American counterpart. Pilate, described as a woman who came

1. Sarah Orne Jewett, *The Country of the Pointed Firs* (1986; rpr. Garden City, N.Y., 1956), 137. Subsequent references in the text are to this edition.

into town "like she owned it," not only is credited with making it possible for Milkman's mother to conceive him by giving her "some greenish-gray grassy-looking stuff" to put in her husband's food, but she is also the one person whose songs and stories teach Milkman how to find meaning in his life.[2] Like Mrs. Todd, Pilate is an example of a female cultural archetype—the priestess figure—a woman equally adept in the natural and spiritual worlds, whose deeds and stories bring healing and knowledge to her community.[3]

In speaking of her fictional characters, Morrison once said, "These are the kind of characters who never had center stage in anybody else's book . . . . Now they're there in all their glory."[4] The characterization of Mrs. Todd and Pilate and the roles they play in their communities suggest that in their fiction Sarah Orne Jewett and Toni Morrison attempt to share cultural resources rooted in myth and folklore that would both inform and trans-

2. Toni Morrison, *Song of Solomon* (New York, 1977), 125. Subsequent references in the text are to this edition.

3. The priestess figure has a mythic analogue in the figure of Demeter. For a recounting of this myth, see Robert Graves, *Greek Myths* (New York, 1955), I, 89–96. For discussions of priestess figures as witch archetypes in women's fiction, see Annis Pratt, *Archetypal Patterns in Women's Fiction* (Bloomington, 1981), 125, 127, 176; Carol Pearson and Katherine Pope, *The Female Hero in American and British Literature* (New York, 1981), 285; Elizabeth Ammons, "Jewett's Witches," in *Critical Essays on Sarah Orne Jewett*, ed. Gwen Nagel (Boston, 1984), 165–84; Sylvia Gray Noyes, "Mrs. Almira Todd, Herbalist-Conjurer," *Colby Library Quarterly*, IX (1972), 643–49. Also see Joseph T. Skerrett, Jr., "Recitation to the Griot: Storytelling and Learning in Morrison's *Song of Solomon*," in *Conjuring: Black Women, Fiction, and Literary Tradition*, ed. Marjorie Pryse and Hortense J. Spillers (Bloomington, 1985), 192–202; and Jacqueline de Weever, "Toni Morrison's Use of Fairy Tale, Folk Tale, and Myth in *Song of Solomon*," *Southern Folklore Quarterly*, XLIV (1980), 131–44. Skerrett refers to Pilate as a priestess shaman figure; de Weever refers to her as the "good witch" and as a "fairy tale creature." All these sources acknowledge women's use of this archetypal figure to suggest the positive cultural function they serve for their community as opposed to the negative image associated with independent, eccentric old women in men's literature.

4. Brian E. Albrecht, "Toni Morrison: Lorain Writer No Slave to Success," Cleveland *Plain Dealer*, April 14, 1981, Sec. B, p. 5.

form the consciousness of their readers. This study is concerned with how the fiction of these two women writers reveals a shared literary aesthetic and narrative intention of cultural affirmation. Both writers seek to affirm what Alice Walker calls the "accumulated collective reality"—the "dreams, imaginings, rituals and legends" that make up the "*subconscious* of a people." Indeed, the call for literary expression based on the folk cultural heritage is familiar in American literature, especially in the words of such writers as Ralph Waldo Emerson, Walt Whitman, Constance Rourke, and Ralph Ellison.[5] Yet, until recently, Jewett and Morrison have traditionally been studied in ways that have invited scholars to overlook, minimize, or negate the cultural material they incorporate into their fiction. Jewett has been discussed in the context of the nineteenth-century local-color movement or regionalism, terms that often reduce the status of her fiction in the established literary canon in much the same way that the context of the black or African-American tradition precludes many white scholars from recognizing how Morrison's fiction both challenges and enriches the canon of the American literary mainstream. Because these two literary contexts are considered mutually exclusive, the cultural and aesthetic concerns that these writers share have gone largely unexplored.

This book attempts to correct this shortsightedness by recognizing myth and folklore as the critical matrix for discussing the fiction of two women who consciously draw on the cultural roots

5. Alice Walker, "From an Interview," in Walker, *In Search of Our Mothers' Gardens* (New York, 1983), 261–62; Ralph Waldo Emerson, "The Poet" (1843), in *Selections from Ralph Waldo Emerson,* ed. Stephen E. Whicher (Boston, 1957), 222–41; Walt Whitman, "Prefaces and Democratic Vistas," in *Complete Poetry and Selected Prose by Walt Whitman,* ed. James E. Miller (Boston, 1959), 455–501; Constance Rourke, *The Roots of American Culture and Other Essays* (New York, 1942), 275–96; and Ralph Ellison, *Shadow and Act* (New York, 1953), 23–73. For an excellent discussion of how many American views on folk expression can be traced to German philosopher and folklorist Johann Gottfried von Herder (1744–1803), see Gene Bluestein, *The Voice of the Folk: Folklore and American Literary Theory* (Amherst, 1972).

or "accumulated collective reality" of their people. Such an approach is possible not only because of the critical space created by recent black and feminist literary scholarship but also because of perspectives like Alice Walker's which raise the possibility that "black and white writers often seem to be writing one immense story . . . with different parts . . . coming from a multitude of different perspectives."[6] Although this study will not overlook or deny the significance of differences between the work of Jewett and that of Morrison, it will focus on the similarities between their literary aesthetics and the presence of storytelling as an activity within their fiction. And it will reveal that in much the same way that Zora Neale Hurston's fiction challenges black people to "unearth the values that could restore the balance . . . and give men and women the words to speak . . . to set their spirits free," the fiction of Jewett and Morrison challenges their readers to be transformed by reaffirming the very values and material the larger culture minimized or devalued.[7]

These writers share a complex response to loss and change in American culture which manifests itself in similar ways. In a sense, Morrison's lament about the loss of archetypal stories echoes the sense of loss Jewett expresses about her native region: "People do not know what they lose when they make away with

6. Alice Walker, "Saving the Life That Is Your Own: The Importance of Models in the Artist's Life," in Walker, *In Search of Our Mothers' Gardens,* 5. Recent scholarship in black and feminist literary theory has begun to clear a critical space for the kind of cross-cultural study I am attempting here. Noteworthy examples include Dexter Fisher, ed., *Minority Language and Literature: Retrospective and Perspective* (New York, 1977); Dexter Fisher and Robert B. Stepto, eds., *Afro-American Literature: The Reconstruction of Instruction* (New York, 1979); Lenore Hoffman and Deborah Rosenfelt, eds., *Teaching Women's Literature from a Regional Perspective* (New York, 1982); Henry Louis Gates, Jr., ed., *Black Literature and Literary Theory* (New York, 1984); and Barbara Bair, "'Ties of Blood and Bonds of Fortune': The Cultural Construction of Gender in American Women's Fiction— An Interdisciplinary Analysis" (Ph.D. dissertation, Brown University, 1984).

7. Cheryl A. Wall, "Zora Neale Hurston: Changing Her Own Words," in *American Novelists Revisited: Essays in Feminist Criticism,* ed. Fritz Fleischmann (Boston, 1982), 391–92.

the reserve, the separateness, the sanctity of the front yard of their grandmothers. It is like . . . [taking] . . . away the fence which, slight as it may be, is a fortification round your home. More things than one may come in without being asked; we Americans had better build more fences than take away from our lives."[8]

Both writers perceive a loss directly related to ideological, economic, and political changes in American life and culture brought on by historical transition. Jewett refers to this transition as the "destroying left hand of progress" that altered late nineteenth-century America by shifting the focus of experience away from rural agrarian areas to the rapidly expanding urban industrial centers.[9] Her reservations about the shift toward modernization echo those of Henry Adams, who questioned "whether the American people knew where they were driving" and observed that "the new American . . . had turned his back on the nineteenth century . . . and had . . . accelerated . . . the . . . brutal consequence of crushing equally the good and the bad." For Morrison, the crucial years of transition were from 1930 to 1950, the period when vast numbers of black Americans migrated from the rural South to the cities of the North. Because she began writing in the 1960s, she surely was also influenced by the turbulence and uneasiness about the loss of roots that came with the press for integration during that period.[10] In the fiction of Jewett and Morrison there is an ambivalence toward the changes the larger culture viewed as "progress."

8. Francis O. Matthiesson, *Sarah Orne Jewett* (Boston, 1929), 31. Also see Annie Fields, ed., *The Letters of Sarah Orne Jewett* (Boston, 1911), 14–15, where Jewett comments on Longfellow's death and losses in general.

9. Susan Willis, "Eruptions of Funk: Historicizing Toni Morrison," in *Black American Literature,* ed. Gates, 263–83; Sarah Orne Jewett, "The River Driftwood," in *Deephaven and Other Stories,* ed. Richard Cary (New Haven, 1966), 175. Subsequent references in the text are to this edition.

10. Henry Adams, *The Education of Henry Adams* (New York, 1931), 343, 349. See Jean Strouse, "Toni Morrison's Black Magic," *Newsweek,* March 30, 1981, pp. 52–57, for a discussion of how events of the 1960s influenced Morrison's fiction.

If this ambivalence seems both positive and negative, then one of the most striking characteristics of Jewett's and Morrison's fictional response to change is that though both writers clearly approve of progress in a general sense, they attempt to reclaim and affirm for fiction parts of their cultural heritage that society had begun to discard as irrelevant or marginal to the dominant national experience. Their efforts resemble a similar effort on the part of nineteenth-century New England poets who, according to Jay Martin,

> helped to continue the past they could still remember into a future which, to most Americans, was as yet dim. They refused to threaten their culture with the new in literature, since Americans were, as they believed . . . too distracted by the new in life. Their values and aspirations, in a middle class American tradition, were consciously conserving, though not necessarily conservative. They were radical enough to be traditional in an age that has spattered tradition with the thin paints of wealth, technology, and science. They were conservators of culture.[11]

Although *radical* is not a term customarily used to describe either Jewett or Morrison, it is appropriate in light of their commitment to affirm that significant cultural materials could be found in places where we least expect them.

Each writer might have followed the literary trends that captured the imaginations of their male contemporaries. Jewett might have written fiction that was more urbane, more cosmopolitan, in the vein of such writers as William Dean Howells and Henry James.[12] Morrison might have focused more directly on the racial

11. See Jay Martin, *Harvests of Change: American Literature, 1865–1914* (Englewood Cliffs, N.J., 1967), 140–44, for a discussion of ambivalence toward progress and historical change in the fiction of New England regionalists. The quotation is on page 13.

12. Perry D. Westbrook, *Acres of Flint: Sarah Orne Jewett and Her Contemporaries* (rev. ed., Metuchen, N.J., 1981), 4. In distinguishing Jewett from Howells and James, I am agreeing with Westbrook that Jewett's realism was more rural in its focus.

and economic oppression of the black urban experience as did such writers as James Baldwin, John A. Williams, and Imamu Baraka (LeRoi Jones). Instead, both Jewett and Morrison consciously chose to reclaim the rural and small-town experience that was being pushed aside or forgotten. As Louis Auchincloss notes in his study of Jewett and eight other American women novelists: "Our women writers . . . have struck a more affirmative note than the men. . . . They have a sharper sense of their stake in the national heritage, and they are always at work to preserve it."[13] In resisting change by affirming the value of cultural artifacts—the customs, manners, language, and stories of commonplace people in commonplace locales—these writers become caretakers or cultural archivists. Thus my first task in this book is to examine separately the historical and cultural contexts out of which Sarah Orne Jewett and Toni Morrison wrote.

Because both perceive themselves as cultural archivists, they choose comparable materials as worthy for fiction. Though Jewett focuses on the rural villages of Maine and Morrison prefers small towns in the Midwest, both comparably depict isolated regional settings or villages and the folk who inhabit them. Of Jewett's fictional materials, Willa Cather remarks: "These stories . . . have much to do with fisher folk and seaside villages; with juniper pastures and lonely farms, neat gray country houses and delightful, well-seasoned old men and women. . . . Miss Jewett wrote of the people who grew out of the soil." Of her own fiction, Toni Morrison explains: "I write what I have recently begun to call village literature, fiction that is really for the village, for the tribe. Peasant literature for *my* people, which is necessary and legitimate but which also allows me to get in touch with all sorts of people."[14] As these statements suggest, both writers not only select village settings but also the attendant mores, customs, beliefs,

13. Louis Auchincloss, *Pioneers and Caretakers: A Study of Nine American Women Novelists* (Minneapolis, 1961), 3.
14. Willa Cather, preface to *Country of the Pointed Firs,* 8; Thomas Le Clair, "The Language Must Not Sweat: A Conversation with Toni Morrison," *New Republic,* March 2, 1981, p. 26.

and language that characterize these settings. And as I will demonstrate, central to each of their fictional projects was the desire to give voice to the unheard through their own oral traditions and narrative discourse.

Writing from an apparent moral imperative, Jewett and Morrison see themselves consciously reclaiming the folklore that their respective cultures either had lost or were about to lose in the wake of dramatic historical change. What occurs, then, is a marriage of their folk knowledge and sensibility to their artistic vision and narrative intention—a marriage that forms what I refer to as their folk aesthetic.[15] As cultural archivists, Jewett and Morrison write from a folk aesthetic that is much like the one that informs Ralph Ellison's theoretical assertion that folklore is the basis of all great literature:

> For us [black Americans] the question should be, What are the specific *forms* of that humanity, and what in our background is worth preserving or abandoning. The clue to this can be found in folklore, which offers the first drawings of any group's character. It preserves mainly those situations which have repeated themselves again and again in the history of any given group. It describes those rites, manners, customs, and so forth, which insure the good life, or destroy it; and it describes those boundaries of feeling, thought and action which that particular group has found to be the limitation of the human condition. It projects this wisdom in symbols which express the group's will to survive. . . . These drawings may be crude but they are nonetheless profound in that they represent the group's attempt to humanize the world. It's no accident that great literature, the products of individual artists, is erected upon this humble base.[16]

15. Elmer Pry, "Folk-Literary Aesthetics in *The Country of the Pointed Firs*," *Tennessee Folklore Society Bulletin*, XLIV (1978), 9–12. Pry's discussion of Jewett's folk literary aesthetics helped inspire my use of the term. I disagree with him that *Pointed Firs* is about the death of a community, but I do agree with his analysis of how folklore functions in the novel.

16. Ellison, *Shadow and Act*, 172.

Although Ellison is specifically referring to the folk base of black literature, his statement captures the general essence of the folk aesthetic that determines both the substance and the structure of Jewett's and Morrison's narrative texts. Thus the second task of this study is to determine how their texts bear witness to their expressed narrative intentions and folk aesthetic.

Yet an examination of the texts themselves shows that these writers are more than mere archivists. They do more than simply collect what the larger culture has attempted to discard, negate, or marginalize. Indeed, they move beyond what Hazel Carby calls a "romantic evocation of the folk" to engage in a vigorous critique of the relationship between "the folk" and American culture.[17] By so doing, they implicitly and explicitly propose a revision of received notions of gender and class and, in Morrison's case, race as well. Jewett's fiction and Morrison's novels reveal that they both seek to challenge the culture's assumptions inscribed in the binary oppositions of rural versus urban people, of old versus young, of the values and traditions of the past versus those of the present, and of male versus female roles and experience. It becomes clear that the goal of their art is not to deny the importance of progress altogether but to challenge those who, in its name, would negate the values embodied in their folk aesthetic. That is, the goal of their art is to redeem or transform their cultures through narrative fiction. This constitutes the second important feature of their complex response to loss and historical change—*i.e.,* they each assume another role, that of "redemptive scribe," a term Richard Cary coined to describe Jewett's determination "to correct the misimpression that native Mainers conformed in type to the caricatured Yankee of fiction." Jewett's conscious assumption of the role of redemptive scribe is apparent in her own formulation of her literary creed: "When I was, perhaps, fifteen, the first city boarders began to make their appearance near Berwick; and the

17. Hazel Carby, *Reconstructing Womanhood: The Emergence of the Afro-American Woman Novelist* (New York, 1987), 175.

way they misconstrued the country people and made game of their peculiarities fired me with indignation. I determined to teach the world that country people were not the awkward, ignorant set those persons seemed to think. I wanted the world to know their grand, simple lives; and so far as I had a mission, when I first began to write, I think that was it." Inherent in Jewett's literary mission is her awareness of narrative's potential to instruct and inform.[18]

Morrison is also a redemptive scribe, for she too takes on a mission to correct a cultural misimpression. As she explains: "Critics generally don't associate black people with ideas. They see marginal people; they just see another story about black folks. They regard the whole thing as sociologically interesting perhaps but very parochial. There's a notion out in the land that there are human beings one writes about, and then there are black people or Indians or some other marginal group. If you write about the world from that point of view, somehow it is considered lesser. It's racist of course. . . . We are people, not aliens. We live, we love and we die."[19] Inherent in Morrison's statement is a desire not only to instruct and inform but to perform a kind of advocacy role, to defend the cultural integrity of her people from those who would perceive narratives about them as marginal and insignificant.

But the label *redemptive scribe* refers to more than the didactic intention of these writers' narrative fiction. It also refers to their desire to bring about cultural transformation. They object to or resist the presumption that the past cannot coexist with the present, that cultural disjunction or discontinuity is a given, that the past must be discarded in the name of progress. Sarah Orne Jewett

18. Richard Cary, introduction to *Deephaven and Other Stories*, 10; Cary, ed., *Sarah Orne Jewett Letters* (Waterville, Maine, 1956), 19–20; also see Cary, *Sarah Orne Jewett* (New York, 1962), 12.

19. Toni Morrison, "Rootedness: The Ancestor as Foundation," in *Black Women Writers (1950–1980): A Critical Evaluation,* ed. Marie Evans (New York, 1984), 121.

and Toni Morrison seek to transform the way their readers perceive the cultural difference of particular people and places as well as the way they interpret the relationship between the past and the present. Instead of emphasizing difference solely, they seek to affirm the value of both difference and resemblance. Instead of discontinuity and opposition between the past and the present, they seek to affirm synthesis, dialogue, and the continuation and survival of the past into the present.[20]

Jewett and Morrison attempt to achieve cultural transformation in three significant ways that connect their roles as cultural archivists and redemptive scribes. First, they attempt to fill the cultural void that they perceive exists in the wake of historical transition. For Jewett, the void was in the lives of those Americans who did not appreciate the cultural wealth to be found in her native New England. For Morrison, the void is in the lives of those black Americans who seem to have lost the oral tradition of storytelling that once sustained a sense of community and enriched their lives. Hence the folk aesthetic in their fiction is a form of cultural intervention. Second, they attempt to endow commonplace people, places, and stories with the mythic grandeur and significance of archetypal narrative and ritual to redeem or rescue neglected literary material and the cultural values on which it is based. I refer to this dimension of their fiction as the mythic impulse. The

20. Rebecca Wall Nail, "Where Every Prospect Pleases: Sarah Orne Jewett, South Berwick, and the Importance of Place," in *Critical Essays,* ed. Nagel, 189. Nail points out that the country/city theme in Jewett's fiction becomes not a matter of opposition or a celebration or rejection, but rather one of dialogue. It seems to me that the same is true for the relationship between the past and the present in her work. Also see Josephine Donovan, *Feminist Theory: The Intellectual Traditions of American Feminism* (New York, 1985), 132–33, for a brief discussion of how French feminists expand on theories of Jacques Derrida to object to such binary oppositions as past/present and country/city. There is a need to deconstruct such oppositions because they actually are a form of "hierarchization which assures the unique valorization of the 'positive' pole." I have chosen a deconstructionist approach to emphasize the dialogue and ambivalence that is inherent in the oppositions in Jewett and Morrison's fiction.

mythic impulse encompasses but is not limited to allusions to classical myth, fairy tale, and the supernatural. It incorporates myth as the "shifting reality" that Claude Lévi-Strauss and J. J. Bachofen remind us it is, but it nevertheless seems to converge around the concept of myth as a collection of stories or beliefs that orient audiences between their "natural" world and the "preternatural" world of possibility.[21] Third, these writers attempt to make narrative a dynamic vehicle for preserving, transmitting, and reshaping the culture in affirmative ways that celebrate the past, that give continuity with the present, and that offer faith in human potential. This third form of transformation involves both writers' use of mythopoesis, the process that Toni Morrison describes as "dusting off the myth" for narrative use. But rather than mere mythical allusion, it involves accommodating mythic archetypes to modern realities and using myth as a "fully accredited mode of ordering human experience."[22]

Both writers seem to confirm Morrison's assertion that "narrative remains the best way to learn anything."[23] This brings us to the third and most important task of this study, which is to show how Jewett's and Morrison's folk aesthetic and the mythic

21. The definition of myth that I use here is derived from my readings in myth criticism and archetypal criticism. On myth, see Claude Lévi-Strauss, *The Raw and the Cooked: Introduction to a Science of Mythology,* trans. John Weightman and Doreen Weightman (New York, 1969), 3; Johann Bachofen, *Myth, Religion, and Mother Right: Selected Writings of J. J. Bachofen,* trans. Ralph Manheim (Princeton, 1967), 76; Richard Chase, *The Quest for Myth* (Baton Rouge, 1949), 97; Joseph Campbell, *The Hero with a Thousand Faces* (Princeton, 1949), 382; Sir James Frazer, *The Golden Bough* (New York, 1951), 824–26; and Mircea Eliade, *Myth and Reality* (New York, 1963). On archetypal criticism see C. G. Jung, "The Psychological Function of Archetypes" and "The Principal Archetypes," in *The Modern Tradition,* ed. Richard Ellmann and Charles Feidelson, Jr. (New Haven, 1964), 648–59; and Northrop Frye, *Anatomy of Criticism: Four Essays* (Princeton, 1957), 131–239.

22. Both Jewett's and Morrison's mythic method (the term is Eliot's) approximates Chase's qualification of the term. See T. S. Eliot, "Ulysses, Order, and Myth," *Dial,* LXXV (November, 1923), 480–83; Chase, *Quest for Myth,* 131, 107; Morrison quoted in Le Clair, "Language Must Not Sweat," 26–27.

23. Le Clair, "Language Must Not Sweat," 26.

impulse operate through narrative to reclaim and affirm cultural difference, to challenge cultural and literary norms, and to demonstrate the dynamic process by which their readers and respective cultures might be transformed.[24] In other words, my thesis is that the fusion of the folk aesthetic and the mythic impulse reveals that narrative in the fiction of Sarah Orne Jewett and Toni Morrison serves a cultural function meant to validate people and places that have been devalued and to offer cultural affirmation of these people and places as a prescription for healing and transforming American culture. Toni Morrison's assertion that the "novel is an art form designed to tell people something they didn't know" suggests that narrative also reminds us of our essential need for a way to make meaning of our individual and collective lives.[25]

Although a concept so basic to human experience as narrative might not ordinarily need definition, the ongoing debate within various disciplines on the "problem of narrative" requires some definition.[26] Robert Scholes and Robert Kellogg define narrative as a literary work distinguished by the presence of a story and a storyteller. It is at the same time a complex process involving four

24. Peter Brooks, *Reading for the Plot: Design and Intention in Narrative* (New York, 1984), xii–xiii.

25. Morrison, "Rootedness," 340. Also see Hayden White, "The Value of Narrativity in the Representation of Reality," in *On Narrative,* ed. W. J. T. Mitchell (Chicago, 1980), 1; and Bruno Bettelheim, *The Uses of Enchantment: The Meaning and Importance of Fairy Tales* (New York, 1977), 3–19.

26. *On Narrative,* ed. Mitchell, vii. My view of narrative is somewhat eclectic because I feel that narrative study has benefited from the plethora of interdisciplinary scholarship, which has enabled us to see connections between narrative, history, folklore, myth, fairy tale, and psychoanalysis. My understanding of these interconnections colors my interpretation of how these writers use narrative. Useful sources on narrative theory include Barbara H. Smith, "Narrative Versions, Narrative Theories," in *On Narrative,* ed. Mitchell, 209–32; Roy Schafer, "Narrative in the Psychoanalytic Dialogue," *ibid.,* 25–49; Robert A. Georges, "Toward an Understanding of Storytelling Events," *Journal of American Folklore,* XXVIII (1969), 313–28; Shlomith Rimmon-Kenan, *Narrative Fiction: Contemporary Poetics* (New York, 1983); Robert Scholes and Robert Kellogg, *The Nature of Narrative* (New York, 1966); and Terry Eagleton, *Literary Theory* (Minneapolis, 1983).

interconnected elements: the story or what is narrated, the story-teller or narrator, the audience (whether it be listener or reader), and the act of storytelling or narrating. Hayden White reminds us that *narrative, narration,* and *to narrate* all derive from the same Latin and Sanskrit roots that mean knowing, to tell, knowable, and known. This etymological perspective is extremely sugges-tive of how I use the term *narrative* here, for I mean two different things at once. First, narrative is a story of complex structure con-sisting of cultural signs—a network of meanings, events, people, places, and things. Second, it is a dynamic process of storytelling as interaction and communication among the interconnected ele-ments of tale, teller, and audience. None of these elements is pas-sive or independent of the others. Instead, as Gerard Genette ar-gues, they are interrelated in narrative discourse. Storytelling as an active process connects the tale with the teller, the teller with the audience, and even the tale with the audience. Like Yeats's dance and dancer, it is difficult to isolate one from the other be-cause together they form an aesthetic whole. Keeping this aes-thetic whole in mind, I will primarily use narrative synonymously with storytelling and story. Related to this definition is the special function narrative serves in the fiction of Sarah Orne Jewett and Toni Morrison. For both writers narrative is a means of affirming the identity of those whose stories have been untold or unheard; it provides information to those seeking knowledge; and it pro-vides healing, transformation, and coherence for the self and the community. Perhaps more important, their fiction helps us see narrative "holistically," as recent poststructuralist critics recom-mend: as an event in which neither the narrator/teller, nor the story/text, nor the audience/listener is a static entity.[27] Instead, all are subject to various transformations during the storytelling event.

27. Scholes and Kellogg, *Nature of Narrative,* 4; White, "Value of Narrativity," 1; Gerard Genette, *Narrative Discourse: An Essay in Method,* trans. Jane E. Lewin (Ithaca, 1980), 25–32; Chase, *Quest for Myth,* 106–107; Georges, "Storytelling Events," 327.

My understanding of these transformations has been greatly helped by recent theoretical perspectives on what Freudian psychoanalysis can teach us about narrative. We traditionally think of narrative as a storytelling event in which a narrator simply recounts a set of happenings. Peter Brooks reminds us that narrative as storytelling is "remembering, repeating and working through." But Roy Schafer's essay on the psychoanalytic dialogue informs us that what is recounted is not a static record but the "present version of the past" in which clarification comes "through the circular and coordinated study of past and present." Thus the narrative as story is in a sense always being transformed. Implicit in this exchange, however, according to Schafer, is the transformation of the narrator, who, in psychoanalytic terms, is "moving forward into new modes of constructing experience." And as recent reader-response criticism reveals, the audience as reader or listener is also transformed in the storytelling event. Wolfgang Iser explains that the reader's "active participation" in the text results in discovery of a "new reality through a fiction which, at least in part, is different from the world he or she . . . is used to; and [of] the deficiencies inherent in prevalent norms and in his or her own restricted behavior."[28] Thus the listener or reader of a narrative is "moving forward in a new mode of constructing experience" and is also thereby transformed.

A network of transformations thus occurs in any given storytelling event. My reading of Jewett and Morrison suggests that these writers were keenly aware of the power of narrative discourse to work these transformations. As cultural archivists, they seem consciously to present situations in which the oral tradition of telling stories is central to the well-being and survival of the

---

28. Brooks, *Reading for the Plot,* 111; Schafer, "Psychoanalytic Dialogue," 32–33; Wolfgang Iser, *The Implied Reader: Patterns of Communication in Prose Fiction from Bunyan to Beckett* (Baltimore, 1974), xii–xiii. See also Susan R. Suleiman and Inge Crosman, eds., *The Reader in the Text: Essays on Audience and Interpretation* (Princeton, 1980); and Jane P. Thompkins, *Reader-Response Criticism: From Formalism to Post-Structuralism* (Baltimore, 1980).

self and of the community. As redemptive scribes, they also seem to suggest that through their narrative texts they could ultimately transform American culture. Indeed, Walter Benjamin's lament about the apparent lack of interest in the oral tradition seems to reflect Jewett's and Morrison's concerns: "The art of storytelling is coming to an end. Less and less frequently do we encounter people with the ability to tell a tale properly. . . . It is as if something that seemed inalienable to us, the securest among our possessions, were taken from us: the ability to exchange experiences." Essentially, both writers remind us of the significant role oral narrative once played in the human story, and they offer their sketches, short stories, and novels as means of filling the void and of perpetuating the "continua of human communication."[29]

In their concern with reclaiming the oral tradition and with using narrative fiction for cultural affirmation and transformation, Jewett and Morrison create American counterparts to the African griots—those village storytellers whom author Alex Haley says "symbolize how all human ancestry goes back to some place, some time where there was no writing. Then, the memories and the mouths of ancient elders was the only way that early history of mankind got passed along." Thus Mrs. Todd in *Pointed Firs* and Pilate in *Song of Solomon* are not just mythic priestesses; as bearers of folk culture, they are also griot figures. In Jewett's *Deephaven* (1877), as the narrator and her friend walk through the village burying ground, the narrator reflects, "We often used to notice names and learn history from the old people whom we knew and in this way we heard many stories which we never shall forget." The link that Jewett makes between the old people of the village and learning the history of a place is similar to the link Morrison makes between the presence of an elder and that figure's "conscious historical connection" with the village or community. Morrison contends that one of the distinctive elements of Afro-

29. Benjamin quoted in José Limon, "Western Marxism and Folklore: A Critical Introduction," *Journal of American Folklore,* XCVI (1983), 34–52; Georges, "Storytelling Events," 327.

American writing is that "there is always an elder there. And these ancestors are not just parents, they are sort of timeless people whose relationships to the character are benevolent, instructive, and protective, and they provide a certain kind of wisdom." She goes on to assert that the presence or absence of that figure determined the success or happiness of the character.[30]

The griot, then, mediates between the self and the community. Perhaps the words of one of the other Dunnet Landing elders in *Pointed Firs,* Mrs. Fosdick, best summarizes the value of the griot figure and the oral narratives she shares: "It does seem so pleasant to talk with an old acquaintance that knows what you know. I see so many of these new folks nowadays, that seem to have neither past nor future. Conversation's got to have some root in the past, or else you've got to explain every remark you make, an' it wears a person out" (58). Mrs. Fosdick's comment suggests that there may be no meaningful future for new folks who have no roots in the past. The griot, however, does not mindlessly recount the past. Instead, the griot has a similar role to that Morrison claims for her novels: to "clarify the roles that have been obscured . . . to identify those things in the past that are useful and those . . . that are not; and . . . to give nourishment."[31]

In sum, this study will focus on narrative as both story and storytelling that operates in the texts of Sarah Orne Jewett and Toni Morrison as a sign of their conscious fictional choices, many of which challenge accepted ideas about women, literature, and commonplace people and places; as a series of storytelling events that recover and reconstruct the past; and ultimately, as a vehicle that can best enable the various audiences within the text, the reader, and the culture at large to be transformed.[32] Moreover, it

30. Alex Haley, acknowledgments to *Roots: The Sage of an American Family* (Garden City, N.Y., 1976), viii; Jewett, *Deephaven,* 66; Morrison, "Rootedness," 343.

31. Le Clair, "Language Must Not Sweat," 26.

32. See Brooks, *Reading for the Plot,* 321, for the use of narrative in psychoanalysis to recover and reconstruct the past.

will show that this use of narrative is achieved through a folk aesthetic and mythic impulse that informs the fiction of both writers. As an index to their artistic vision and narrative intention, the folk aesthetic will be discussed in terms of how it reconstructs the folk community through vernacular language and expressions; how it represents the oral traditions of storytelling and gossip; how it focuses on the value of female experience; and how it affirms commonplace rather than middle-class values.[33] As an index to the desire of both Jewett and Morrison to endow everyday people, places, and things with a larger-than-life quality, the mythic impulse appears in allusions to classical myth (and in Morrison's case, African-American and classical myth); in modern reconstructions of myths to express desire, transcendence, wish-fulfillment and freedom; in mythic patterns of questing, ceremony, and ritual; and in poetic dramatizations of the intersection of the real and the supernatural.

Although others have acknowledged some elements of myth and folklore in the fiction of these two writers, little attention has been given to how the folk aesthetic and mythic impulse fuse in their works or to what this fusion achieves for their fiction.[34]

33. See Pry, "Folk-Literary Aesthetics," 8, for his list of ways folklore functions in *Pointed Firs*.

34. On the use of myth and folklore in Jewett, see Pry, "Folk-Literary Aesthetics"; Ammons, "Jewett's Witches"; Theodore R. Hovet, "Once Upon a Time: Sarah Orne Jewett's 'A White Heron' as a Fairy Tale," *Studies in Short Fiction,* XV (1978), 63–68; and Sarah Sherman, "Victorians and the Matriarchal Mythology: A Source for Mrs. Todd," *Colby Library Quarterly,* XXII (1986), 63–74. Sherman's more recent study, *Sarah Orne Jewett: An American Persephone* (Hanover, 1989), offers an excellent comprehensive analysis of Jewett's use of myth and traces Jewett's interest in the Demeter-Persephone myth to Walter Pater and her mentor and friend Annie Fields. For Morrison, see Cynthia A. Davis, "Self, Society, and Myth in Toni Morrison's Fiction," *Contemporary Literature,* XXIII (1982), 333–42; Grace Ann Hovet and Barbara Lounsberry, "Flying as Symbol and Legend in Toni Morrison's *The Bluest Eye, Sula,* and *Song of Solomon," CLA Journal,* XXVII (December, 1983), 119–40; de Weever, "Toni Morrison's Use of Fairy Tale"; Leslie A. Harris, "Myth as Structure in Toni Morrison's *Song of Solomon," MELUS,* VII (1980), 69–82; and Morrison, "Rootedness," 339–45.

I will attempt to pull these elements together for each writer separately and to suggest that Jewett's and Morrison's fiction reveals
similar narrative intentions and aesthetic visions. Such an approach, based on a close reading of selected texts, can offer a new
way of connecting separate strands of American culture and literary expression. In her familiar but often undervalued study *The
Roots of American Culture,* Constance Rourke calls attention to the
need for writers and critics alike to bring new approaches to the
American landscape. As she puts it: "A prodigious amount of
work is still to be done in the way of unearthing, defining, and
synthesizing our traditions, and finally in making them known
through simple and natural means. Beneath this purpose must
probably lie fresh constructions of our notion as to what constitutes a culture, with a removal of ancient snobberies and with new
inclusions."[35] Even after four decades, her words are still prophetic, though recent scholarship, especially in feminist and black
literary criticism, has begun the unearthing and synthesis she calls
for. The connections and reconstructions that I present in this
cross-cultural study make a possible new paradigm for opening
the canon of literary criticism to include other studies of how
black and white women writers use folklore, myth, and narrative
in their fiction.

Although I argue that myth and folklore constitute an important critical matrix in Sarah Orne Jewett's and Toni Morrison's use
of narrative, I also recognize that neither writer is independent of
other literary contexts. Rather, for both of them realism is the
other important critical matrix.[36] Ironically, this generic identifi-

35. Rourke, *Roots of American Culture,* 295.
36. *Critical Essays,* ed. Nagel, 1. Useful sources on American literary realism
and local color include Edwin H. Cady, *The Road to Realism: The Early Years
(1837–1885) of William Dean Howells* (Syracuse, 1956); Josephine Donovan, *New
England Local Color Literature: A Woman's Tradition* (New York, 1983); Ann Douglas Wood, "The Literature of Impoverishment: The Women Local Colorists in
America, 1865–1914," *Women's Studies,* I (1972), 3–46; Gwen L. Nagel, ed., *Sarah
Orne Jewett: A Reference Guide* (Boston, 1978); and Warner Berthoff, *The Ferment
of Realism: American Literature, 1884–1919* (New York, 1965).

cation is qualified in similar ways for both. Jewett's term *imaginative realism* is very similar to the *magical realism* so often applied to Morrison.[37] Although the inclusion of folk materials may initially signal a reductive mimetic realism to some readers, both of these qualifications of the genre suggest how the fiction of each writer surpassed the limitations of realism as a literary convention. Josephine Donovan's assertion that for Jewett the term "suggests a dimension beyond the real" echoes William Dean Howells' early praise for her ability to imbue her sketches "with a true feeling for the ideal within the real." In one of her letters, Jewett comments on the meaning of the term *imaginative realism:* "You bring something to the reading of a story that the story would go very lame without; but it is those unwritable things that the story holds in its heart; if it has any, that make the true soul of it, and these must be understood, and yet how many a story goes lame for the lack of understanding." The term is also implied in an entry in her diary in 1871 that expresses what was to become one of the most important tenets of her literary credo: "Father said this one day, 'A story should be managed so that it should *suggest* interesting things to the *reader* instead of the author's doing all the thinking for him, and setting it before him in black and white. The best compliment is for the reader to say "why didn't he put in 'this' or 'that.' " ' "[38]

Morrison expresses a related concern for the reader when she explains that she seeks to "provide the places and spaces so that

37. Fields, ed., *Letters of Jewett,* 112, and Cary, ed., *Jewett Letters,* 69. Also see Jean Boggia-Sola, "The Poetic Realism of Sarah Orne Jewett," *Colby Library Quarterly,* VII (1965), 74–81. In R. Z. Sheppard's review of the book *Conversations with American Writers* by Charles Ruas, "Quiet Please, Writers Talking," is a reference to Morrison's attempt "to evoke black history with the techniques of magic realism" (*Time,* December 24, 1984, pp. 68–69). Also see Skerrett, "Recitation to the Griot," 192, and Dorothy H. Lee, "*Song of Solomon:* To Ride the Air," *Black American Literature Forum,* XVI (1982), 64–70. Morrison herself, however, has never used this term to describe her fiction.

38. W. D. Howells, "Review of *Deephaven,*" in *Critical Essays,* ed. Nagel, 25–26 (also see Josephine Donovan, *Sarah Orne Jewett* [New York, 1980], 134–35); Fields, ed., *Letters of Jewett,* 112; Cary, ed., *Jewett Letters,* 69.

the reader can participate." But in another statement Morrison more precisely describes her form of realism: "I . . . blend the acceptance of the supernatural and a profound rootedness in the real world at the same time with neither taking precedence over the other. It is indicative of the cosmology, the way in which Black people look at the world. We are very practical people, very down-to-earth, even shrewd people. But within that practicality we also accepted what I suppose could be called superstition and magic, which is another way of knowing things." On one hand, Morrison's blend of African-American cosmology and epistemology calls traditional definitions of realism into question and reveals how her use of the convention differs from Jewett's. On the other hand, Morrison's words remind us that all definitions of realism are shaped by complex ideological, historical, and cultural contingencies of value that blur commonplace distinctions between what is real and what is not.[39]

Yet Jewett's blend of the "ideal within the real" and Morrison's suffusion of magic over a "rootedness in the real world" are representative of how the use of realism connects these two writers. In fact, the very nature of these two forms of realism makes possible the fusion of the folk aesthetic and mythic impulse. They also remind us of the two maxims of Gustave Flaubert that inspired Jewett's literary creed, which instruct the writer "to write everyday life as one writes history" and "not to make one laugh, but to act the way nature does—that is, to make one dream." Ironically, as Louis Renza points out, because of the conditions that determined women's cultural production at the end of the nineteenth century Jewett had to mediate her desire to write "life as one writes history" against a complex set of historical relations and literary conventions that worked against the literary ambitions of women writers. Hence the "unwritable things" of her fiction are as significant to this study as those that are explicitly inscribed in her texts.[40]

39. Quoted in Donovan, *Jewett,* 4; Morrison, "Rootedness," 341–42.
40. Fields, ed., *Letters of Jewett,* 165; Martin, *Harvests of Change,* 147–48. Louis A. Renza, *"A White Heron" and the Question of Minor Literature* (Madison, 1984),

At the time that Sarah Orne Jewett began her literary career, the American landscape was undergoing the economic and social changes that would determine her use of realism. She assesses these changes in the 1893 Preface to *Deephaven*. Her reaction to the burgeoning wealth, rising industrialism, and growing alienation between "townspeople and country people"(32) was to write fictional sketches and novels that spoke to the values she saw vanishing. In her words, "tradition and time-honored custom were to be swept away . . . by the irresistible current" (32). Implicit in this opinion is both a critique of and a challenge to the values that accompanied urban industrialization:

> Character and architecture seemed to lose individuality and distinction. The new riches of the country were seldom very well spent in those days; the money that the tourist or summer citizen left behind him was apt to be used to sweep away the quaint houses, the roadside thicket, the shady woodland, that had lured him first; and the well-filled purses that were scattered in our country's first great triumphal impulse of prosperity often came into the hands of people who hastened to spoil instead of to mend the best things that the village held. It will remain for later generations to make amends for the sad use of riches after the war, for our injury of what we inherited, for the irreparable loss of certain ancient buildings which would have been twice as interesting in the next century. (33)

Ann Douglas Wood might have read this passage as support for her thesis that the women local-color writers such as Jewett had a limited vision; I maintain that the opposite is true. Rather, their view was broad enough to accommodate an alternative way of representing women and neglected regions of the American landscape in fiction. They did not seek a nostalgic retreat to the past

---

142–68, provides an excellent deconstructive analysis of Jewett's fiction in relation to her status in the American literary canon and the cultural and literary milieu in which she wrote.

as some have suggested. Instead, they sought to reclaim both the good and the bad that characterized these regions. Thus their regionalism is not a "genteel evasion of the more complex if not sordid social realities of American life," as Renza claims. In fact, Jewett maintains that "a dull country village is just the place to find the real drama of life."[41]

Toni Morrison also wrote at a time of historical and cultural change. She saw black Americans losing many of the cultural values and the sense of tradition that had sustained them before the massive migration from South to North. In her fiction she consciously seeks to incorporate the language and these lost or forgotten traditions:

> The novel tells about the city values, the urban values. Now my people, we "peasants," have come to the city, that is to say, we live with its values. It's confusing. There has to be a mode to do what the music did for blacks, what we used to be able to do for each other in private and in that civilization that existed underneath the white civilization. I think this accounts for the address of my books. I am not explaining anything to anybody. My work bears witness and suggests who the outlaws were, who survived under what circumstances and why, what was legal in the community as opposed to what was legal outside of it. All of that is in the fabric of the story in order to do what the music used to do. The music kept us alive, but it's not enough anymore. My people are being devoured.[42]

Like Jewett, Morrison does not lament the past but seeks a means of reclaiming what is good and useful to empower her people to survive difficult circumstances in the present. Such a connection for her, and indeed for Jewett, was essential to their survival and that of their respective communities. And just as Jewett had to

41. Wood, "Literature of Impoverishment," 17; Renza, "White Heron," 44–45; Donovan, *Jewett,* 134.

42. Morrison quoted in Le Clair, "Language Must Not Sweat," 26; Willis, "Eruptions of Funk," 263–83.

begin within the context of the local-color movement of her time but sought to expand the literary restrictions inherent in that movement to fit her own aesthetic vision, Morrison seeks to use the novel in an African-American context, in a "black way." Hence she continues to incorporate the oral tradition of the black literary tradition in her fiction. In her words, she wants her fiction to be "both print and oral literature . . . to make the story appear oral, meandering, effortless, spoken." Her desire is consistent with what Robert Stepto says is the best African-American literature—it presents the gift of a "historical and linguistic portrait of a culture once imprisoned by an enforced illiteracy—questing for, finding, and relishing the written word."[43] Ultimately, she seeks to offer narrative fiction to foster connections within the community, to focus on shared experience and the affirmation of cultural identity in the context of national diversity, to be both an archivist and a redemptive scribe for her people.

Even the earliest works of Jewett and Morrison reveal the folk aesthetic, mythic impulse, and cultural function of narrative that would characterize their best works. The folk aesthetic in Jewett's *Deephaven* illustrates how the consciousness of two young urban women is transformed through the storytelling sessions they share with the denizens of the rural community they visit. Although the transformation is not nearly as convincing as it is in *Pointed Firs,* Jewett nevertheless reveals how the women begin to discard condescending attitudes toward rural people and locales. The mythic impulse in Morrison's *Bluest Eye* illustrates the tragic consequences of growing up with "Dick and Jane" stories, plotless narratives of sterile existence and shallow values that distort the consciousness of a young black girl. The absence of black cultural narratives destroys the consciousness and even the sanity of the protagonist in Morrison's first novel. By the time each author wrote her most acclaimed work, she brought the folk aesthetic

---

43. Morrison, "Rootedness," 341; Robert B. Stepto, "Teaching Afro-American Literature: Survey or Tradition—The Reconstruction of Instruction," in *Afro-American Literature,* ed. Fisher and Stepto, 23.

and mythic impulse into greater balance. That is, both authors continued to write from an aesthetic based on the folk traditions of their respective cultures, but they began to rely to a larger extent on the value of mythic patterns to reveal the unique grandeur and cultural significance of those traditions to their readers. I associate this balance of the folk aesthetic and the mythic impulse with the two distinct cultural drives that give life meaning—the need for roots and the "wish for wings."[44]

The cross-cultural approach I take in this book is an effort to link two women writers whose ethnic backgrounds, narrative themes, and cultural and literary contexts might initially seem to preclude any possibility of similarities. Indeed, the differences are not only obvious but too significant to overlook. To do so would be both reductive and dismissive. By drawing on recent scholarship in such areas as literary folklore, myth criticism, narrative theory, African-American literary theory and criticism, and feminist criticism, I seek to offer a way of examining the unexpected similarities in their expressed literary concerns and their textual productions. Jewett's desire to "acquaint the people of a region with one another" and Morrison's commitment "to tell people something they didn't know" reveal similar narrative intentions to subvert well-established literary conventions and to affirm what American culture had devalued, marginalized, or forgotten. Yet I do not seek to submerge the respective narrative intentions of these authors into a neutralizing discourse of universality. To do so would be to minimize the very cultural specificity that each writer attempts to affirm in her fiction.[45] Instead, I argue that their respective literary and cultural circumstances prompted them to engage in analogous literary projects. Their textual productions were not reactionary responses to these circumstances but power-

44. Nina Auerbach, *Woman and the Demon: The Life of a Victorian Myth* (Cambridge, 1982), 111–12.

45. See Jessica Benjamin, *The Bonds of Love: Psychoanalysis, Feminism, and the Problem of Domination* (New York, 1988), 183–218, for a brilliant analysis of how "universal discourse" simultaneously hides yet reifies cultural domination.

ful forms of cultural intervention. They were at once radical forms of resistance to cultural domination and radical affirmations of women and their respective communities and cultural traditions. Most important, they bear witness' to the cultural function of narrative to alter our perspective and transform our consciousness. A connection of this sort can provide what Alice Walker describes as the "unifying theme through diversity, a fearlessness of growth, of search, of looking that enlarges the private and public worlds."[46] The chapters that follow attempt to enlarge these two worlds by examining how Sarah Orne Jewett's and Toni Morrison's use of folklore and myth affirms that narrative can offer not a ready-made construct or escape from change but a dynamic vehicle for our individual and collective journeys.

46. Walker, "Saving the Life," in Walker, *In Search of Our Mothers' Gardens,* 5.

I

RITUALS OF FLIGHT AND RETURN:
THE CYCLICAL JOURNEYS OF JEWETT'S
FEMALE CHARACTERS

> Without ever leaving the ground she could fly.
> —Toni Morrison, *Song of Solomon*

> Our life is an apprenticeship to the truth that around every
> circle another circle can be drawn; that there is no end in
> nature, but every end is a beginning.
> —Ralph Waldo Emerson, "Circles"

One of the primary signs of the mythic impulse in Sarah Orne
Jewett's fiction is the nature of the journeys her female characters
undertake.[1] Whether they retreat from the hurried life of the cities
for the presumed tranquillity of country villages or flee from the
idyllic quietude of the country for the sophisticated lure of the
city, the women in Jewett's narratives continually contemplate or
embark on journeys outside the confines of the place they call
home. In light of Jewett's expressed affection for the rural villages
of Maine, the journey from city to country is not surprising, but
the journey from country to city is. Indeed, it might seem in-
consistent that she so often uses flight imagery to describe the real
and imaginative journeys of her country women. Though seemingly contradictory, this characteristic imagery bespeaks an ironic
affirmation of her native region, a celebration of its self-reliant

---

1. This chapter is a revised and expanded version of a paper I delivered at the
Sarah Orne Jewett conference held at Westbrook College in 1985. As later chapters
will demonstrate, motifs of flight are profoundly significant in Morrison's fiction
as well. The paper was subsequently published as "Rituals of Flight and Return:
The Ironic Journeys of Sarah Orne Jewett's Female Characters," *Colby Library
Quarterly*, XXII (1986), 36–42.

women, and a recognition of their desire to transcend the "narrow set of circumstances [that] . . . caged [them] . . . and held [them] . . . captive."[2] By employing this imagery to describe the journeys of her female characters, she challenges the cultural notions that "range is masculine and confinement is feminine."[3] Later, when we turn to Toni Morrison's fiction, we will see not only how she draws on the uses of flight that are indigenous to African-American literature but also how she challenges cultural assumptions about women and about human potential through flight imagery in ways that are analogous to Jewett's.[4] Both writers draw on the wealth of associations implicit in flight, which varies from flight as freedom and escape to flight as transcendence and self-actualization.[5]

In Jewett's fiction, flight symbolism is signified not only in obvious references to flying, fleeing, and flitting but in numerous allusions to birds, excursions, and journeys. Although a different form of flight predominates in each text, certain patterns emerge from her attempt to acquaint her readers with the range of experience available to her New England women.[6] Indeed, the pattern

2. Jewett, *Pointed Firs*, 95. Rebecca Wall Nail ("Where Every Prospect Pleases," 185–98) asserts that Jewett both "loves and rejects" her native region. I see more affirmation than rejection.

3. Mary Ellmann, *Thinking About Women* (New York, 1968), 87. Ellmann says these two notions were a natural law that became a social and cultural axiom when it was repealed in the late nineteenth century.

4. Hovet and Lounsberry, "Flying as Symbol," 119–40.

5. J. E. Cirlot, *A Dictionary of Symbols*, trans. Jack Sage (London, 1977), 109. Mircea Eliade contends that the desire for "imaginary universes in which space is transcended and weight is abolished" has its roots in the depths of the human psyche, which explains why it is intrinsic to the myth and folklore of so many different cultures. According to Hindu culture, "Among all things that fly, the mind is the swiftest" and "Those who know have wings." See Eliade, *Myth, Rites, Symbols: A Mircea Eliade Reader,* ed. Wendell C. Beane and William G. Doty (2 vols.; New York, 1975), I, 233–43.

6. See Fields, ed., *Letters of Jewett,* 228, and Jewett, *Deephaven,* 31–32, for Jewett's comments on Plato's dictum that "the best thing that can be done for the people of a state is to make them acquainted with one another."

of flight and mobility of her female characters is in sharp contrast
to what Nina Auerbach refers to as the "familiar cult of home"
usually associated with the lives of Victorian women.[7] The most
significant of these patterns—the flight to the outside world and
the inevitable return home—have the mythic characteristics of
ritual and reveal Jewett's complex response to this region, to its
women, and to her own role as a regional writer.

If we were to view the journeys of her women from the traditional perspective of the male quest in American literature, their
returns would appear to signify aborted journeys or truncated experiences that overshadow and negate the liberating mobility that
precedes them.[8] Yet, although inevitable, the return at the end of
the female quest is not a resignation to limitation or failure but a
heroic expression of the desire to remain connected to the people
and place of her cultural roots. In other words, it is an act of triumph, of self-affirmation and communal celebration.[9] But herein
lies both the complexity and the irony of these journeys, for
though they are the journeys of coping women, they nevertheless
implicitly point to a larger culture that no longer appreciates the
values, traditions, or experiences of these rural women's lives. The
focus of this chapter, then, is on how the cyclical journeys of

7. Auerbach, *Woman and the Demon,* 124–25; Barbara Johns, "'Mateless and
Appealing': Growing into Spinsterhood in Sarah Orne Jewett," in *Critical Essays,*
ed. Nagel, 147–75.

8. Useful discussions on the male quest in American literature include Bair,
"'Ties of Blood,'" 32–63; Leslie Fiedler, *Love and Death in the American Novel* (rev.
ed.; New York, 1966); Sam Bluefarb, *The Escape Motif in the American Novel: Mark
Twain to Richard Wright* (Columbus, 1972); Kathryn Allen Rabuzzi, *The Sacred and
the Feminine: Toward a Theology of Housework* (New York, 1982); Donovan, *Feminist Theory,* 171–215; Nina Baym, "Melodramas of Beset Manhood: How Theories of American Fiction Exclude Women Authors," *American Quarterly,* XXXIII
(1981), 123–39.

9. Toni Morrison asserts that "when the hero returns to the fold (in Afro-
American literature)—returns to the tribe—it is seen by certain white critics as a
defeat, by others as a triumph, and that is a difference in what the aims of art are."
I believe Jewett sees the return for female characters in a similar way. See Morrison,
"Rootedness," 343–44, and Sherman, *Sarah Orne Jewett,* 189–224.

Jewett's female characters function in three ways: as rituals of flight and return; as ironic manifestations of her folk aesthetic and mythic impulse; and, ultimately, as devices around which to structure narratives that could bring about the transformed consciousness she sought for her readers.[10]

In Sarah Orne Jewett's fiction, rituals of flight and return most often involve the journey from the country to the city and back. But Jewett uses the "visitor motif" in which a cosmopolitan outsider journeys from the city to the country and back to the city in her first book, *Deephaven,* and also in *The Country of the Pointed Firs,* the masterpiece that evolved from it nineteen years later.[11] In *Deephaven,* Jewett structures a series of sketches around the journey of two young women from Boston to the country village of Deephaven.[12] Their journey is a flight in the sense that they regard the trip to Deephaven as an opportunity to abandon their adult female roles for the carefree playfulness of young girls. As Kate Lancaster explains in trying to entice her friend Helen Denis to accompany her on this summer retreat, "It might be dull in Deephaven for two young ladies who were fond of gay society and dependent upon excitement, I suppose; but for two little girls who were fond of each other and could play in the boats, and dig and build homes in the sea sand, and gather shells, and carry their

10. Elizabeth Ammons, "Going in Circles: The Female Geography of Jewett's *Country of the Pointed Firs,*" *Studies in the Literary Imagination,* XVI (Fall, 1983), 83–92. Also see Josephine Donovan, "Sarah Orne Jewett's Critical Theory: Notes Toward a Feminine Literary Mode," in *Critical Essays,* ed. Nagel, 212–25.

11. For critical opinions on the visitor motif, see Robert L. Horn, "The Power of Jewett's *Deephaven,*" *Colby Library Quarterly,* IX (1972), 617; Paul John Eakin, "Sarah Orne Jewett and the Meaning of Country Life," *American Literature,* XXXVIII (1967), 523; Catherine Barnes Stevenson, "The Double Consciousness of the Narrator in Sarah Orne Jewett's Fiction," *Colby Library Quarterly,* XI (1975), 2; and Margaret Ferrand Thorp, *Sarah Orne Jewett* (Minneapolis, 1966), 31.

12. Critical opinion is mixed as to whether *Deephaven* is a book of sketches or a novel. I discuss it as a novel because of the consistent narrative point of view, overall structure, and unity although it lacks some of the coherence we expect of a novel. See John Eldridge Frost, *Sarah Orne Jewett* (Milford, N.H., 1960), 149; Cary, *Appreciation of Sarah Orne Jewett,* x; Donovan, *Jewett,* 31–32.

dolls wherever they went, what could be pleasanter?"(38). In referring to themselves as girls, though they are both twenty-four years old, Kate suggests that their journey is an escape or at least a temporary reprieve from adulthood and the need to conform to societal expectations.[13] It is also a flight from a dependence on the urban attractions they associate with life in Boston. They assume that Deephaven, by contrast, will offer opportunities for recreation, independence, and freedom. Thus not only is their journey a flight, but by enabling them to regress emotionally into childhood, it is also a return. Once Kate and Helen arrive in Deephaven, however, they cannot totally escape into child's play. Instead, they must confront both the pleasant and unpleasant realities of this rural landscape and its people. *Deephaven,* as narrated by Helen, is Jewett's first attempt at deconstructing the preconceived notions about country life that these two visitors, as representatives of an urban perspective, held dear.

The girls confront the realities of country life through a series of departures from and returns to the Brandon House, a symbol of the dignified past of the aristocracy that becomes the communal hub of the village. It can be argued that the focus of *Deephaven* is more on these miniature journeys within the village than on the larger journey from the city to the country. According to Ann Romines, these journeys within Deephaven are a "series of abrupt, abortive encounters with ritual" in which the girls try out local rites as sympathetic spectators rather than empathic participants.[14] On one hand, it seems that Romines makes a valid distinction in contrasting the "encounters with ritual" in *Deephaven* with the more profound experiences with ritual that occur in *Pointed Firs.* Kate and Helen never seem to become immersed in the life of the milieu but remain friendly outsiders. Thus their

13. Donovan, *Jewett,* 32–33.

14. Ann Romines, "In *Deephaven:* Skirmishes Near the Swamp," *Colby Library Quarterly,* XVI (1980), 205–19. The term *empathic* is from Marcia McClintock Folsom, "'Tact is a Kind of Mind-Reading': Empathic Style in Sarah Orne Jewett's *The Country of the Pointed Firs,*" in *Critical Essays,* ed. Nagel, 76–89.

journeys do seem to be encounters rather than experiences. Often their reactions to much of what they see, hear, and feel seem to be expressed in sentimental tones of the very condescension Jewett seeks to dispel. For example, as the girls return from the Brandon House after sharing in the ritual of prayer and Scripture reading at the home of the Carews, the narrator reacts to ritual with sophisticated detachment: "We told each other, as we went home in the moonlight down the quiet street, how much we had enjoyed the evening, for somehow the house and the people had nothing to do with the present or the hurry of modern life. I have never heard that psalm since without its bringing back that summer night in Deephaven, the beautiful quaint old room, and Kate and I feeling so young and worldly, by contrast, the flickering shaded light of the candles, the old book, and the voices that said Amen"(76). If we assume that Jewett's primary focus is on the education of the two visitors, then it might seem that their youth and worldly sophistication prohibit them from appreciating the significance or complexity of the ritual or from moving beyond the connotation of terms such as *quaint*.

On the other hand, when we take a closer look at *Deephaven* and remember that it is Jewett's first book, we must acknowledge it as the work of a writer struggling to illuminate the nature of the rituals themselves. Thus what Romines dismisses as "ritual as spectator sport" or "sympathetic voyeurism" is really a consequence of Jewett's attempt to focus first on the essence of the rituals and the country folk who participate in and sustain them and only secondarily on the visitors who observe them or only marginally participate in them.[15] In other words, at the incipient stage of her literary career, the folk aesthetic takes precedence over but does not exclude character development. And because Jewett's efforts to wed the two are tenuous, one might overlook the subtle ways in which the text leads us to recognize how the consciousness of the narrator is transformed. Thus Jewett's somewhat un-

15. Romines, "In *Deephaven*," 210.

wieldy narrative execution causes some readers and critics to misconstrue her motives for writing the sketches that make up the book.[16]

There is no better statement of her motives than the 1893 Preface to *Deephaven* in which she writes:

> The younger writer of these Deephaven sketches was possessed by a dark fear that townspeople and country people would never understand one another, or learn to profit by their new relationship. She may have had the unconscious desire to make some sort of explanation to those who still expected to find the caricatured Yankee of fiction. . . . Small and old-fashioned towns, of which Deephaven may, by the reader's courtesy, stand as a type, were no longer almost self-subsistent, as in earlier times; and . . . many a mournful villager felt the anxiety that came with these years of change. Tradition and time-honored custom were to be swept away together by the irresistible current. (32)

Jewett's phrase "tradition and time-honored custom" may be interpreted as a reference to ritual. This prefatory statement, then, is an expression of her narrative intention to redirect the current of historical change, a current Jewett refers to as the "destroying left hand of progress" that she feared was nullifying the rituals she associated with village folk.[17] Hence *Deephaven* is not merely a genteel portrait of quaint country life but a conscious attempt to preserve in fiction the complexity of the rituals that give continuity and coherence to a people and their way of life.[18] Moreover, the Preface to *Deephaven* not only provides the reader with a statement of her narrative intentions, but it also identifies Jewett with the folk or "mournful villagers" at the same time that it gives her the narrative detachment she needs.

16. Horn, "Power," 617.

17. Jewett, "The River Driftwood," in *Deephaven*, 175.

18. For an excellent account of Jewett's awareness of the literary pioneering inherent in her fiction, see Renza, *"White Heron,"* 43–72.

Deephaven and the rest of Jewett's fiction exhibit a shifting narrative stance that seems to mirror the frequent journeys her characters undertake. This emphasis on mobility can be attributed to Jewett's career-long concern with acquainting city and country people. As Francis O. Matthiessen points out, Jewett was "hoping that *Deephaven* might help people to look at 'commonplace' lives from the inside instead of the outside, to see that there is so deep and true a sentiment and loyalty and tenderness and courtesy and patience where at first sight there is only roughness and coarseness and something to be ridiculed."[19] Although the narrator of *Deephaven* never claims kinship with her rural neighbors, as does the narrator of *Pointed Firs* whom she prefigures, she does gradually lose her original interest in carefree self-indulgence and begins to develop a genuine interest in the village folk of Deephaven. For the reader, such signs of growth and transformation signify revised attitudes toward country people and country ways. Moreover, they are a consequence of the narrator's observation of and participation in the rituals of the Deephaven village.

I prefer to interpret the "encounters with ritual" not as flaws in the narrative but as conscious literary devices for depicting the feminine rituals of country life and for revealing how exposure to these rituals could transform the consciousness of an individual. Of all the various rituals that are depicted in Jewett's fiction, storytelling is the most significant, and in *Deephaven* it figures strongly in each of the journeys the visitors make from the Brandon House. Their journey to the home of Mrs. Patton, also known as the Widow Jim, is an opportunity not only to learn more about her but about the entire village community. As a priestess and herbalist who preserves village culture through her sharp memory and refined narrative ability, she shares stories that encourage the narrator and her friend to abandon their preconceived notions about country people and places. Appropriately, it is Mrs. Patton who is the principal caretaker of Brandon

19. Matthiessen, *Sarah Orne Jewett*, 51–52.

House, the literal and symbolic repository of the relics of the past. It is also Mrs. Patton who "knew everybody's secrets" and who "had either seen everything that . . . happened in Deephaven for a long time, or had received the particulars from reliable witnesses" (61–62).

She relishes visits from Kate and Helen as opportunities to "rec'lect" and share bits of gossip, news, and wisdom (64). Moreover, the description of her reveals a female character who illustrates the oral tradition of regional folklore. The narrator observes: "There must be her counterpart in all old New England villages. . . . She was commander-in-chief at . . . funeral[s] and . . . she had all genealogy and relationship at her tongue's end. . . . She chattered all day to you as a sparrow twitters, and you did not tire of her; Kate and I were never more agreeably entertained than when she told us of old times and of Kate's ancestors and their contemporaries; for her memory was wonderful"(61–63). Clearly, Mrs. Patton exemplifies the ritual of storytelling at its best. As a virtual female New England griot, she is one of the most valuable members of the community, not only for the visitors but also for those for whom Deephaven is home. Storytelling has value for her in that it allows her to journey into memory, reaffirm the experiences that shaped her life, and celebrate the triumph over these experiences, no matter how difficult or painful. Her recollections offer a path into an appreciation of the life she represents. Jewett seems to posit the ritual of storytelling as a folk art whose significance resides in its value for the teller as well as the listener.

The significance of storytelling as ritual is apparent in other ways as well. When the girls visit the Deephaven burying ground, the narrator reflects on its value for acquainting them with the past and present of Deephaven: "We often used to notice names and learn their history from the old people whom we knew, and in this way we heard many stories which we shall never forget. It is wonderful, the romance and tragedy and adventure which one may find in a quiet old-fashioned country town, though to heartily enjoy the everyday life and character, one must find plea-sure in thought and observation of simple things, and have an instinctive, delicious interest in what to others is unflavored dull-ness" (66). Though it is questionable whether the narrator had this "instinctive, delicious interest" in country life before her visit to Deephaven, it is clear that she gradually develops an appreci-ation for the region every time she observes or participates in its rituals. Storytelling has become a means of discovering facets of country life that an urbane outsider might otherwise overlook or minimize. Jewett seems to suggest that only through such a ritual is it possible to discover the intrinsic vitality of the rural landscape.

Beneath this image of storytelling is a narrative tension that is difficult to ignore. One source of this tension may be Jewett's am-bivalence toward her native region, but I believe the complexity of this tension indicates two sources that are a great deal more significant.[20] One of these is Jewett's ironic affirmation of both the positive and negative dimensions of country life. Ironic affirma-tion differs from ambivalence in that the writer is not simply torn by two contrary aspects of a subject but recognizes that the pres-ence of these contrary aspects is what enriches that subject. Hence Deephaven takes on greater value because Jewett's narrator ac-knowledges the "adventure" that lies in the "romance" *and* the "tragedy" of Deephaven. Consequently, her perspective toward it cannot remain narrow or condescending. The other source of nar-rative tension is inherent in the very nature of storytelling as a literal and symbolic act. Just as each journey between the Brandon House and the lighthouse represents a new adventure, each story-telling experience represents a new journey into yet another "ver-sion" of the story of Deephaven life. As narrative critic Barbara H. Smith observes, "For any particular narrative, there is no single *basically* basic story subsisting beneath it but, rather, an un-

20. See Mobley, "Rituals of Flight and Return"; Warner Berthoff, "The Art of Jewett's *Pointed Firs*," *New England Quarterly*, XXX (March, 1959), 31–53; Eakin, "Jewett and the Meaning of Country Life"; Nail, "Where Every Prospect Pleases."

limited number of any other narratives that can be *constructed in response* to it or perceived as *related* to it."[21] Storytelling, then, is not a closed but an open act that by its very nature presupposes various other versions subsisting at once. Kate and Helen discover this through their exchanges with Mrs. Patton, Captain Lant, Captain Sands, and numerous other old people of Deephaven. Through each of their stories, Jewett challenges received cultural notions that would construct their several stories into one or would limit the New England character to a single monolithic type.

On a symbolic level, storytelling is a circular journey that involves a return to the past to recollect and retell a particular tale. Thus each recollection and retelling links the past with the present. It is also a ritual that links the old to the young in Jewett's fiction. Recollections of the past and the "esteem for the wisdom of age" are recurring motifs in Jewett that signify "time as a single continuum," contrary to the prevailing attitude of her time that the country life of villages such as Deephaven were anachronistic vestiges of an earlier and no longer relevant era.[22] As a ritual, storytelling unites the teller, tale, and listener, creating a collective memory that connects the self to a community of others. An example of the communal value of storytelling is apparent in the chapter "The Captains," in which the girls visit Captain Lant, one of the several "ancient mariners," as the narrator calls them, whose seafaring days survive only in memories and daily narrative exchanges with fellow captains: "We asked him many questions about the old people and found he knew all the family histories and told them with great satisfaction. We found he had his pet stories, and it must have been gratifying to have an entirely new and fresh audience. He was adroit in leading the conversation

21. See Smith, "Narrative Versions." Also see Seymour Chatman, "What Novels Can Do That Films Can't (and Vice Versa)," in *On Narrative,* ed. W. J. T. Mitchell (Chicago, 1980), 117–36.

22. Mary C. Kraus, "Sarah Orne Jewett and Temporal Continuity," *Colby Library Quarterly,* XV (1979), 157–74.

around to a point where the stories would come in appropriately, and we helped him as much as possible. In a small neighborhood all the people knew each other's stories and experiences by heart. . . . There was a story which he told us . . . which . . . seems to me worth preserving" (80–81). Not only does this passage affirm the value of shared narratives for giving coherence to a community, but with the words "in a small neighborhood, all the people know each other," Jewett once more evokes narrative tension. This time the tension derives from an implicit comparison of the affirmation of storytelling as a communal bond and the subtle acknowledgment that historical changes such as urbanization, which may represent progress, can also irrevocably alter the life of small locales and threaten the bonds that hold them together. In short, the narrative tension that characterizes the ritual of storytelling in *Deephaven* is not tension in a negative sense. It is, rather, a consequence of Jewett's desire to "restore the balance" to the image of a particular people in a particular place through her folk aesthetic.

The "Cunner Fishing" chapter, in which the girls share an extended storytelling session with Captain Sands, presents three additional dimensions of storytelling that exemplify Jewett's folk aesthetic at the same time that they signify her mythic impulse. These three dimensions are the narrative technique of the frame story, the vernacular or folk language used in telling the stories, and the "imaginary initiation" that storytelling engenders for the listener.[23] My purpose in exploring these dimensions is to suggest that despite some obvious flaws, *Deephaven* has a great deal more narrative complexity than has traditionally been recognized.

23. See Eliade, *Myth and Reality,* 136, 138, 202. Quotation from Ursula K. LeGuin, "It Was a Dark and Stormy Night; or, Why Are We Huddling About the Campfire?" in *On Narrative,* ed. Mitchell, 193. The term *imaginary initiation* is related to the empathic style that Marcia Folsom describes. In Jewett's fiction, storytelling reduces the distance between listener and teller by fostering empathy in the listener for the storyteller's experience. See Folsom, "'Tact Is a Kind of Mind-Reading,'" 76–89.

In adopting the frame story or story-within-a-story technique, Jewett is, of course, using a fairly old literary convention. I compare this technique to concentric circles. If we consider the outer circle as the story of Helen, the narrator, then Captain Sands's story is a circle inside of hers, and the stories he tells become circles within his. The common center of each of these circles is the portrait of Deephaven they all help to create. The pattern recurs throughout the book, but the girls spend so much time with Captain Sands, described as "one of the most prominent citizens of Deephaven" (93), who had "most decided opinions on dreams and other mysteries, and [who] could tell some stories which were considered incredible by even a Deephaven audience" (121), that it is appropriate to devote some attention to the contribution of their encounters with him to the text of *Deephaven*. We can interpret the outer rim of any single circle as the path of flight and return that the narrator takes from the present into the past and back again. This pattern is most graphic with Captain Sands, who is felt to be so much apart from the present that he "had a reputation in town for being peculiar and somewhat visionary" (93). The point is, however, that his flights of imagination and narrative enrich his own life and those of the two visitors. As the narrator of stories within the narrator's story, Captain Sands serves both as community poet and village historian. In one of his narratives, he recounts: "Everything's changed from what it was when I used to follow the sea. I wonder sometimes if the sailors have as queer works aboard ship as they used. Bless ye! Deephaven used to be a different place to what it is now; there was hardly a day in the year that you didn't hear the shipwright's hammers, and there was always something going on at the wharves. You would see the folks from up country comin' in with their loads of oak knees and plank, and . . . the men flapping their arms to keep warm, and hallooing as if there wasn't nothin' else goin' on in the world except to get them masts to the shipyard" (115). This account and numerous others ranging from tales of the sea to personal narrations about Captain Sands's wife, father,

and grandfather and his own psychic visions demonstrate Robert
Scholes's assertion that "not what really happened but the meaning of what the narrator believes to have happened becomes the
central preoccupation of this kind of narrative."[24]

The stories of Captain Sands are also valuable for their generous supply of folk expressions. This linguistic element—the use
of the vernacular or folk language—is another significant dimension of the storytelling rituals, not in the local-color sense of cari-
cature or entertainment but as a sign of Jewett's desire to give
voice to the folk. In other words, there are instances in the text
when the girls find the characteristic language of the region enter-
taining, but from these we can infer that Jewett simply seeks to
illustrate the typical reaction of outsiders to folk speech. More
significantly, Jewett's use of Maine vernacular is a sign of her folk
aesthetic in that this language reveals what Elmer Pry refers to as
the "folk erudition" and wisdom that gives authority to those
who use it.[25] When Captain Sands uses expressions such as "The
Devil is whipping his wife" (121) to explain the appearance of the
sun during rainfall, or proverbs such as "A growing moon chaws
up the clouds" (114), he reveals that he is conversant with the
common body of beliefs and knowledge that connects the people
of the region. When he assures Kate and Helen of the veracity of
his stories with the words "I'm telling you the living truth" (126),
he is using an idiomatic expression to establish the authority behind his words. He further establishes the authority of his words
through the folk wisdom inherent in knowledge that is at once
intuitive and experiential, metaphysical and earthly. An example
of Captain Sands's folk knowledge is evident when he interrupts
the narration of one of his own stories to speculate about the mysteries of life:

> I says to myself, "Well, I always was given to understand that when
> we come to a futur' state we was going to have more wisdom than we
> can get afore." . . . "It's the thinking that does it" says I, "and we've

24. Scholes and Kellogg, *Nature of Narrative*, 261.
25. Pry, "Folk-Literary Aesthetics," 9.

got some faculty or other that we don't know much about. We've got some way of sending our thought like a bullet goes out of a gun and it hits. We don't know nothing except what we see. And some folks is scared, and some more thinks it is all nonsense and laughs. But there's something we haven't got the hang of." . . . I guess we shall turn these fac'lties to account some time or 'nother. Seems to me, though, that we might depend on 'em now more than we do. (123–24)

Here Jewett's use of the vernacular or oral tradition is not only a sign of her folk aesthetic but also a means of character development. Captain Sands is portrayed not as a strange old man but as a wise elder capable of profound insights into human nature.

The text of *Deephaven* is replete with examples of the oral tradition. In the language of Mrs. Patton, Captain Sands, or Mrs. Bonny, whose folk idioms, stories, and expressions are some of the best in the book, Jewett's folk aesthetic gives depth to the portrait of country people. At one point the narrator's reflections on the storytelling of Captain Sands suggests the value of the oral tradition: "The captain was under full sail on what we heard was his pet subject, and it was a great satisfaction to listen to what he had to say. It loses a great deal in being written, for the old sailor's voice and gestures and thorough earnestness all carried no little persuasion. And it was impossible not to be sure that he knew more than people usually do about these mysteries in which he delighted" (124). The oral tradition, in the form of storytelling, provides a journey for both the teller and the listener. And in the implied narrative intervention, Jewett suggests that the reader is a part of this journey as well, though he or she cannot fully appreciate the subtle intricacies of the spoken word once it is given a written form.[26]

26. In making the distinction between an oral and a written story, Jewett is using a subtle form of narrative intervention that Robyn R. Warhol argues is typical of much nineteenth-century fiction. It occurs in varying degrees of subtlety throughout *Deephaven* and occasionally in some of the short stories. For her excellent analysis of this technique, see Warhol, "Toward a Theory of the Engaging Narrator: Earnest Interventions in Gaskell, Stowe, Eliot," *PMLA*, CI (1986), 811–18.

This brings us to the most important dimension of storytelling in Jewett's fiction, and that is in the "imaginary initiation" that the folk aesthetic and mythic impulse engender for the listener. I borrow this term from Mircea Eliade, who writes that "believing that he is merely amusing himself or escaping, the man of the modern societies still benefits from the imaginary initiation supplied by tales." [27] The term is suggestive of the gradual transformation that the narrator undergoes in shedding naive preconceptions and adopting a more enlightened appreciation for the experiences of others. Though the following passage is sometimes dismissed as sentimental or melodramatic, it nevertheless points to this new insight that comes from listening to the tales of Deephaven residents:

> I believe old Captain Sands is right, and we have instincts which defy all our wisdom and for which we can never frame laws. We may laugh at them, but we are always meeting them. . . . I wonder . . . why it is that one hears so much more of such things from simple country people. . . . There is one side of such lives for which one cannot help having reverence; they live so much nearer to nature than people who are in cities, and there is a soberness about country people often times that one cannot help noticing. . . . In their simple life they take their instincts for truths, and perhaps they are not always so far wrong as we imagine. (130–31)

Although this insight borders on being Cooperesque and stereotypical, [28] it nevertheless suggests some degree of change in the

27. Eliade, *Myth and Reality*, 136, 138, 202. Imaginative initiation is very similar to vicarious initiation. Initiation, as the term implies, is rarely a physical journey but often an imaginative trip into the "foreign" territory of a narrative. See LeGuin, "It Was a Dark and Stormy Night," 193.

28. By *Cooperesque* I mean in the tradition of James Fenimore Cooper and the generally acknowledged critical view of his portraiture of Native Americans and country folk. This form of stereotyping is evident in a passage at the end of the "Mrs. Bonny" section, where the narrator reflects, "There was something so wild

narrator's consciousness. One of the most telling signs of the imaginary initiation is the carryover into the conversation of the narrator and her friend when they return to the Brandon House later that evening. Not only does their earlier storytelling session with Captain Sands inspire them to discuss his stories and the mysteries of which he spoke, but even more important, it inspires them to recall, recite, and interpret the Greek myth of Demeter and Persephone. This passage deserves to be quoted at length:

> "Do you remember in the old myth of Demeter and Persephone," Kate asked me, "where Demeter takes care of the child and gives it ambrosia and hides it in fire, because she loves it and wishes to make it immortal, and give it eternal youth; and then the mother finds it out and cries in terror to hinder her, and the goddess angrily throws the child down and rushes away? And he had to share the common destiny of mankind, though he always had some wonderful inscrutable grace and wisdom, because a goddess had loved him and held him in her arms. I always thought that part of her story beautiful where Demeter throws off her disguise and is no longer an old woman, and the great house is filled with brightness like lightning, and she rushes out through the halls with her yellow hair waving over her shoulders, and the people would give anything to bring her back again, and to undo their mistake. I knew it all by heart once . . . and I am always finding new meaning in it. I was just thinking that it may be that we all have given to us more or less of another nature, as the child had whom Demeter wished to make like the gods. (130)

In addition to being a sign of Jewett's conscious attempt to connect folk and mythic narratives, the allusion to the myth of Demeter

---

and unconventional about Mrs. Bonny that it was like taking an afternoon walk with a good-natured Indian" (139).

and Persephone is significant for several other reasons.[29] Some of these are related to how the girls interpret the myth; others are related to what the myth itself suggests.

In the first place, Kate begins her retelling of the myth with an almost rhetorical question, "Do you remember . . . ?" and proceeds to share her own remembrance of the myth. She thus engages in a kind of flight from the present moment to return to a received narrative from her childhood. She enters the myth not at the beginning but in the middle with her reference to Demophoon, the child Demeter attempts to make immortal. When she reflects on the myth at this particular retelling of it, what has meaning for her is not the characters of Demeter and Persephone per se, but the child, who, despite the lost opportunity for immortality and eternal youth, possesses a numinous quality similar to that of the goddess who loved him. Thus, although the myth is one recalled from her childhood, her interpretation of it reveals that the narrative is not static but dynamic and subject to the narrator, the time, and the circumstances. Hence it virtually becomes a new "version." Kate connects the numinous quality of the child to the mysterious wisdom or "powers which are imperfectly developed in this life" (130) but which occasionally manifest themselves in people like Captain Sands. The reference to such powers prompts the narrator to wonder "why it is that one hears so much more of such things from simple country people . . . [who] believe in dreams . . . have a kind of fetichism [sic] and believe so heartily in supernatural causes" (130).

Apparently, although both girls have heard and retold this myth many times in the past, on this occasion, inspired by the folk narratives of Deephaven, it evokes a new interpretation.

29. Useful summaries and interpretations of the myth of Demeter and Persephone include Graves, *Greek Myths;* Thomas Bullfinch, *Bullfinch's Mythology* (New York, 1978); Walter Pater, "The Myth of Demeter and Persephone," *Fortnightly Review,* January–February, 1876; Bachofen, *Myth, Religion, and Mother Right;* Pratt, *Archetypal Patterns;* and Sherman, "Victorians and the Matriarchal Mythology."

Kate's new understanding helps her appreciate country people, who, she says, "have much in common, after all, with the plants which grow up out of the ground and the wild creatures which depend upon their instincts wholly" (131). Kate's new response to the myth demonstrates her greater sense of connection with country people and a new appreciation of the spiritual essence in nature: "I think . . . that the more one lives out of doors the more personality there seems to be in what we call inanimate things. The strength of the hills and the voice of the waves are no longer only grand poetical sentences, but an expression of something real, and more and more one finds God himself in the world, and believes that we may read the thoughts He writes for us in the book of Nature. And after this we were silent for a while" (131). The meditative and even metaphysical dimension of this passage reminds us of Jewett's expressed admiration for the theosophy of Emanuel Swedenborg, of which she writes: "I keep a sense of it under everything else. How such a bit of foundation lifts up all one's other thoughts together, and makes us feel as if we really stood higher and could see more of the world."[30] The personal sensation of transcendence that Jewett describes here is very similar to the feeling she ascribes to her protagonists as they contemplate the meaning of the myth of Demeter and Persephone.

In their moment of contemplation they experience a transformation of consciousness. At this point in their journey into Deephaven, they have taken flight in a more profound sense than their original flight from the city and adulthood. Here they leave present time and space and return to a narrative of their childhood, which in turn inspires a flight resembling what Patricia Meyer Spacks terms "a kind of escape through imagination."[31] And again we have an example of how the ritual of storytelling inspires

30. Fields, ed., *Letters of Jewett*, 21–22. See also Donovan, *New England Local Color Literature*, 100–101. For an overview of Swedenborg's thought, see Sig Synnestvedt, *The Essential Swedenborg: Basic Teachings of Emanuel Swedenborg, Scientist, Philosopher, and Theologian* (New York, 1970).

31. Patricia Meyer Spacks, *The Female Imagination* (New York, 1975), 411.

an imaginary initiation. Thus Jewett forces us to reexamine our customary criticism of the desire to return to childhood as a negative form of escape from maturity. She invites us to consider instead how such a return might be a reverse initiation—a growth into the openness of childhood that accepts freedom over limitations, diversity over conformity, discovery over prejudice. Inherent in this reexamination is Jewett's challenge to the male quest or initiatory experience associated with a boy becoming a man.

But the myth of Demeter and Persephone suggests even more. Because we associate Demeter, the goddess of agriculture and fertility, with nature, we can interpret the journey of Kate and Helen to Deephaven as an archetypal return to nature. We can even interpret their residence in the city as analogous to Persephone's rape and captivity in the underworld. Thus the visits to the elderly, especially the old women, appear analogous to the mother-daughter reunion of Demeter and Persephone. Furthermore, as an enactment of the ritualistic return and departure of spring, summer, and fall, the telling and retelling of the Demeter-Persephone myth become a ritual of affirmation of the cycle of life, which links women to nature.[32] Deephaven becomes a "haven" or refuge, where a spiritual rebirth can occur.

Although I maintain that storytelling is a most important ritual in *Deephaven,* it is by no means the only one. The girls observe and participate in other rituals as well—churchgoing, herb gathering, gossiping, and calling on neighbors. Two other rituals of particular interest are the circus at Denby, which they attend, and a "walking funeral," which they observe (148). The girls begin to realize that the journey to the circus is almost more important than the circus itself when they observe the "straggling train of carriages which had begun to go through the village . . . and they started on the journey shouting and carousing" (99). Mrs. Kew, the keeper at the lighthouse, accompanies the girls, and it is through her that they register further "the importance of the oc-

32. Pratt, *Archetypal Patterns,* 125–26.

casion" for Deephavenites (100). But the occasion loses much of its excitement when they arrive at the tent of the giantess, the four-hundred-pound woman whom the narrator considers an "absurd, pitiful creature" as the circus freak or sideshow (106). The significance of the giantess' personal history in taking on that role is that it represents another dimension of Deephaven life—the story of a woman's life and the vicissitudes of having a drunken father, of becoming poor, and of losing her ambition. The significance of the walking funeral is that it shows the girls how country people regard death. As they leave the house to begin the walking procession to the burying ground, the narrator observes:

> Before the people had entered the house, there had been . . . an indifferent, business like look, but when they came out, all that was changed; their faces were awed by the presence of death, and the indifference had given place to uncertainty. Their neighbor was immeasurably their superior now. Living, he had been a failure by their own low standards; but now, if he could come back, he would know secrets, and be wise beyond anything they could imagine. . . . There came a sudden consciousness of the mystery and inevitableness of death. . . . And there was a thought, too, of the limitation of this present life; we were waiting there, in company with the people, the great sea, and the rocks and fields themselves, on this side of the boundary. We knew just then how close to this familiar, everyday world might be the other, which at times before had seemed so far away, out of reach of even our thoughts. (148–49)

This passage is from the chapter appropriately titled "In Shadows," the twelfth of *Deephaven*'s thirteen chapters. We are reminded of Persephone's annual journey to the shadows of the underworld and of the cycle of life that Jewett seeks to affirm even as she calls attention to its tragedies. Once more we see not only how ritual teaches Kate and Helen about country people and country life but how it presents a new opportunity for them to expand their own consciousness and to become aware of their connection to a segment of humanity they once patronized with detachment, curiosity, or condescension.

The end of *Deephaven* is somewhat problematic because it openly calls into question much of what Jewett seems to have affirmed. For example, Kate briefly fantasizes about remaining in Deephaven year-round but consoles herself with the thought that "village life is not stimulating, and there would not be much to do in winter" (160). The narrator admits that they would "think it a hard fate, and not enjoy it half so much" if they really belonged to Deephaven (160). Consequently, Jewett implicates both the reader and the narrator in a voyeuristic gaze at each other, a gaze that undermines the process of acquiring the transformed consciousness she seeks to achieve. In a sense, this is the narrative tension referred to earlier, in which Jewett seems to say yes and no to this landscape at one and the same time. It seems, however, that Jewett recognizes and even wants to lessen this tension when Kate says: "I have understood something lately better than I ever did before,—it is that success and happiness are not things of chance with us; but of choice. I can see how we might easily have had a dull summer here. Of course, it is our own fault if the events of our lives are hindrances; it is we who make them bad or good. Sometimes it is a conscious choice, but oftener unconscious. I suppose we educate ourselves for taking the best of life or the worst" (160–61).

The journey to Deephaven has not only educated Kate and Helen to appreciate their own freedom of choice but to recognize that same freedom among country people. Thus the two protagonists have undergone a gradual and even subtle transformation. They have become less frivolous and more reflective, less sympathetic and more empathetic. By listening to and sharing in the stories of Deephaven, they have journeyed from ignorance and condescension to an enlightened appreciation of cultural difference. Moreover, they have gained a new perspective toward the inherent strength of a village that has chosen to accept and cope with change rather than be defeated by it. Kate expresses their new attitude in these words: "Dear ol Deephaven! . . . I don't dispute the usefulness of a new, bustling, manufacturing town with its progressive ideas; but there is a simple dignity in a town like Deephaven, as if it tried to be loyal to the traditions of its ancestors. It quietly accepts its altered circumstances . . . and has no harsh feelings toward the places which have drawn away its business, but it lives on" (161).

The freedom to journey to a new place is a privilege the girls realize they have to a greater degree than their Deephaven friends. Yet the journey to this particular place has enlarged their vision, transformed their consciousness, and enriched their memories. The return to Boston at the end of the book represents a flight from the irreconcilable differences between country and city life, but it is also a flight into the deep recesses of their memory, which enables them to continue their journey and to celebrate and affirm the vitality of life they bear witness to in Deephaven. *Pointed Firs* foregrounds this same pattern of cyclical journeys that give structure to Jewett's narratives, that celebrate the rituals of country people for the affirmation of self and community they engender, and that demonstrate her mythic impulse to reveal what the transcendent grandeur of country folk could teach us about life and living.

With the exception of *Pointed Firs,* "A White Heron" (1886) represents the most dramatic example of Jewett's flight motifs.[33] The portrayal of Sylvia is an exquisitely complex sketch of a young girl's initiatory journey into womanhood—a journey that occurs simultaneously on three levels: physically, as an actual adventure; imaginatively, as a "voyage" of discovery; and symbolically, as a passage from ignorance to knowledge. Although the story begins with a description of her as content and secure within her rural setting, Sylvia craves more space than her grandmother's home provides. Consistent with the pastoral resonances in her

33. All parenthetical references in the text to "A White Heron," "The Flight of Betsey Lane," "The Hiltons' Holiday," and *Pointed Firs* are to the 1956 edition.

name is her grandmother's description of her as a "great wand'rer" (164) with whom wild creatures and birds could easily identify.[34] Thus on one hand it might seem to be simply a tale of a naive girl who must choose between the familiar pastoral world in which she resides and the world of romantic love and money to which the young hunter belongs. Annis Pratt refers to the pastoral setting we identify with Sylvia as the "green world."[35] On the other hand, because Sylvia decides to remain in her idyllic green world setting, a decision informed by her physical and imaginative flight out of her environment, she emerges from her dilemma as a heroic, mature young woman in one sense, yet a perpetual child in another. To clarify the ironic complexities of her decision, it is useful to analyze Sylvia from three perspectives: her existence before her journey, her initiatory journey, and her return to the farm. These perspectives help to define the extent to which Sylvia's initiation is a success.

Sylvia is first described as "a little girl," which immediately distinguishes her from most of Jewett's other female characters, who are elderly. Though she lives with her grandmother, she is portrayed as an isolated character whose only real companion is "a plodding, dilatory" (161) old cow. Even though she considers her home a "beautiful place to live," she nevertheless craves more space than the farm affords her. Her grandmother notes that there "never was such a child for straying about out-of-doors" (162), and to their guest she explains that, like her son, Sylvia is one for whom "there ain't a foot a ground she don't know her way over, and the wild creatur's counts her one o' themselves" (164–65). These passages establish the adventuresome innocence and the smothering narrowness of Sylvia's existence as a yet uninitiated girl. The young male visitor, an ornithologist, provides an oppor-

34. Pearson and Pope, *Female Hero*, 21–23. This study points out that the comparison or identification of women with birds occurs frequently in women's literature.
35. Pratt, *Archetypal Patterns*, 125–26.

tunity for her not only to flee her environment but also to undertake a journey of initiation.

When the young man tries to entice Sylvia to assist him in finding the prized heron for his collection, Sylvia is described in terms
that suggest the beginning of an initiation experience: "She could
not understand why he killed the very birds he seemed to like so
much. But as the day waned, Sylvia still watched the young man
with loving admiration. She had never seen anybody as charming
and delightful; the woman's heart, asleep in the child, was vaguely
thrilled by a dream of love" (166). Even more significant than
the "dream of love" the ornithologist arouses is the "spirit of
adventure . . . [the] wild ambition . . . [the] fancied triumph and
delight and glory" (167) that would be hers should she discover
the heron's nest. Thus in this story Jewett juxtaposes the male and
female versions of the quest. Whereas Sylvia appears to live in
communication with nature, the ornithologist represents an intrusion into nature that violates the order and signals a break in the
harmonious calm of this essentially female landscape.[36] Jewett is
again introducing the visitor motif into her fiction, but for entirely different reasons than in *Deephaven,* for example. She employs the traditional nineteenth-century convention of using a
male figure to shape the occasion for a woman's narrative at the
same time she revises that narrative to critique the incongruities
in what Marianne Hirsch calls "heterosexual plots."[37]

As a visitor, the ornithologist is the outsider, who not only
does not observe or participate in the rituals of this landscape but
seems to be virtually oblivious to them in his eagerness to locate

36. More than one critic has noted that the ornithologist represents a male
intrusion into a virtually female landscape. For discussions of this idea, see Pratt,
Archetypal Patterns, 19; Renza, *"White Heron,"* 64–65; Elizabeth Ammons, "The
Shape of Violence in Jewett's 'A White Heron,'" *Colby Library Quarterly,* XXII
(1986), 6–16; Donovan, *New England Local Color Literature,* 107–109; and Richard
Brenzo, "Free Heron or Dead Sparrow: Sylvia's Choice in Sarah Orne Jewett's
'A White Heron,'" *Colby Library Quarterly,* XIV (1978), 36–41.

37. See Marianne Hirsch, *The Mother/Daughter Plot: Narrative, Psychoanalysis,
Feminism* (Bloomington, 1989), 5, 102–103.

the heron's nest. His intrusion into the landscape poses a threat to nature and to the very order that sustains the milieu. Although he listens eagerly to the grandmother's "quaint talk" (165), he does not notice the "hint of family sorrows" (165) in her conversation, for "his eager interest" is on snaring the white heron. Thus a form of narrative tension emerges from the positive voyage his appearance inspires for Sylvia against the potential for violence that he symbolizes.

Concerned with more than merely finding the nest, she thinks with greater excitement of the vantage point she would gain by climbing the old pine tree that towers above all the others. She is aware that "if one climbed it at break of day . . . one [could] see all the world" (167). And therein lies her challenge. The journey she must embark upon is more an upward than an outward one, a direction that emphasizes not only the limits of her environment but points to her affinity with the bird, a common comparison in women's literature.[38] Because the journey is an upward one, it symbolically suggests the restricted range of experience available to Sylvia. One is reminded again of the cultural axiom that distinguishes how range and confinement apply to men and women. Yet, because she negotiates mobility in spite of her confinement and because her birdlike flight allows her to see above and beyond her environment, encoded in the journey is a freedom she is experiencing for the first time. This journey ultimately affects her decision and determines the course of her life thereafter.

If the "dream of love" is short-lived, it is because Sylvia's desire to reach the vantage point where she can "see all the world" (167) is not just a desire for more space but a desire for the spiritual transcendence Jewett associates with Swedenborg. Thus Sylvia does not consider the journey up the tree as a dangerous physical feat but as a rewarding flight to a greater range of experience, freedom, and knowledge. In language customarily attributed to the heroism of male characters and male quests, Jewett captures

38. Pearson and Pope, *Female Hero,* 21–23.

the overall spirit of adventure and struggle that characterizes Sylvia's quest:

> Small and hopeful Sylvia began with utmost bravery to mount to the top . . . with tingling, eager blood coursing the channels of her whole frame, with her bare feet and fingers, that pinched and held like bird's claws to the monstrous ladder. . . . When she made the dangerous pass from one tree to the other, the great enterprise would really begin. . . . The tree seemed . . . like a great main-mast to the voyaging earth . . . [to] this determined spark of human spirit. . . . The solitary gray-eyed child . . . stood trembling and tired but wholly triumphant, high in a tree-top. . . . Then Sylvia, well-satisfied, makes her perilous way down again. (168–70)

Although the sexual connotations of this passage are fairly obvious, it seems to me that the broader connotations of heroic struggle, of dangerous adventure, and of fulfilling triumph are more significant. In that the word *utmost* connotes a comparison, Jewett makes a distinction between what is accepted as bravery in the larger culture and an apparently superior form of that bravery. Louis A. Renza asserts that this seemingly conscious appropriation of male language and male connotations outlines an "exclusive feminine declaration" against male literary authority.[39] This feminine declaration extends to the two epiphanies that occur at the height of Sylvia's journey. The first is the feeling that, like the birds, "she too could go flying" (169), and the second is her feeling of triumph upon discovering the secret nest of the white heron.

The nature of her triumph—successfully making the solitary passage from ignorance to knowledge of the world—rehearses the traditional metaphor for the initiatory experience in American literature. As Ihab Hassan defines it in *Radical Innocence:* "Initiation can be understood . . . as the first existential ordeal, crisis or en-

39. Renza. *"White Heron,"* 74–115.

counter with experience in the life of a youth. Its ideal aim is knowledge, recognition, and confirmation in the world, to which the actions of the initiate, however painful, must tend. It is, quite simply, the viable mode of confronting adult realities."[40] In the context of a confrontation with adult realities, however, Sylvia's initiatory journey is both a success and a failure. In some ways her journey corresponds to the traditional pattern of the initiation journey—separation or departure, trial or ordeal, communication of communal secrets, and a return to the community—but in other ways it does not.[41] She confronts the reality of her environment, symbolized by the painful, rigorous climb, and ventures beyond it to acquire the knowledge of the outside world she once only dreamed of, but she nevertheless withdraws from this world and returns, by choice, to the protection of her grandmother's farm. In this sense, her journey is more imaginative than real, more symbolic than realistic. Moreover, her knowledge fails to prepare her for dealing with the realities the hunter represents; consequently her departure seems both complete and abortive.

Indeed, if we were to focus solely on the flight or departure, it might seem that Sylvia is simply another character who attempts to "transcend" what Josephine Donovan describes as the boredom and isolation of rural life with which Jewett was so familiar.[42] Instead, Sylvia's return and refusal to reveal communal secrets is a departure from the traditional initiation pattern. Sylvia's refusal to reveal the location of the heron's nest confirms that the journey gives her not only knowledge of the outside world but also courage to reject that world and protect her own. Thus, just as her

40. Ihab Hassan, *Radical Innocence: Studies in the Contemporary American Novel* (New York, 1961), 41.

41. Virginia Sue Brown Machann, "American Perspectives on Women's Initiations: The Mythic and Realistic Coming to Consciousness," *Dissertation Abstracts International*, XL (1979), 1470A.

42. Josephine Donovan, "A Woman's Vision of Transcendence: A New Interpretation of the Works of Sarah Orne Jewett," *Massachusetts Review*, XXI (1980), 366.

journey has been a heroic act, so is her decision to deny "the great world . . . for a bird's sake" (170–71). Because Sylvia is identified with the bird, her decision is for her own sake as well. Moreover, it is a liberating experience that empowers her, through both the acts of expansion and denial, to affirm her own freedom and to protect the sanctity of nature against the destructive values of the hunter. The distinction that A. M. Buchan draws between male and female writers, a distinction possibly open to question, nevertheless aptly describes the difference between the hunter's attitude toward nature and Sylvia's: "The woman writer . . . need not go out consciously to seek since much that she gathers in this search will remain foreign to her. She must work with materials that memory and affection have made her very own, whether or not they appear trifling in the eyes of the world. She creates not like a man, subduing the objects of the earth to his arrogant purpose and recording them vaingloriously, but like a woman, guarding and perpetuating within herself the essential human values."[43] Not only does Sylvia guard "essential human values," but she perpetuates the harmonious relationship with nature.

Ironically, however, in guarding these values, she simultaneously appears to sacrifice her social and emotional development as a woman, at least as this development is culturally defined. Her decision to remain on the farm might be considered a rejection of the larger world of experience—the world of mature, romantic love. Thus, at the same time that she is a coping female hero, she could also be regarded as a perpetual child. What seems on one level to be a rite of passage of a young girl into adolescence if not womanhood appears on another level to be an abortive journey from ignorance to knowledge back to the comfort of a green world, Edenic setting. Sylvia's ritual of flight and return may be seen not so much as a "coming of age," for she is only nine years old, as a growing into consciousness or an awareness we might

43. A. M. Buchan, *Our Dear Sarah: An Essay on Sarah Orne Jewett* (St. Louis, 1942), 45.

call spiritual transcendence.[44] The sign of this transcendence appears in the description of her at the height of her flight just before her descent back to the ground: "She stood trembling and tired but wholly triumphant, high in the tree-top. . . . Sylvia felt as if she too could go flying among the clouds. . . . Truly it was a vast and awesome world" (169).

Sylvia's epiphanic experience resembles Jewett's description of the unique sensation of being in harmony with nature: "When one goes out of doors and wanders about alone at such a time, how wonderfully one becomes part of nature, like an atom of quicksilver against a great mass. I hardly keep my separate consciousness."[45] Thus "A White Heron" seems to posit the value of a spiritual knowledge that comes from a communion with nature over more temporal ways of knowing and being in the world.

It is probably the conclusion more than any other part of the story that has invited so many and often conflicting interpretations of this American classic. At the end of the story, when Sylvia returns from her journey, she finds her grandmother and the hunter standing together in the doorway waiting "to hear the story she can tell." A possible explanation for Sylvia's choice "not to speak after all" but to "keep silence" is posed:

> No, she must keep silence! What is it that suddenly forbids her and makes her dumb? Has she been nine years growing, and now, when the great world for the first time puts out a hand to her, must she thrust it aside for a bird's sake? The murmur of the pine's green branches in her ears, she remembers how the white heron came flying through the golden air and how they watched the sea and morning together, and Sylvia cannot speak; she cannot tell the heron's secret and give its life away. (170–71)

The above passage, and indeed the entire story, is so replete with allegorical resonances that the reader is invited to speculate be-

44. Machann, "American Perspectives on Women's Initiations." See also Donovan, "Woman's Vision," 365–80.
45. Fields, ed., *Letters of Jewett,* 51.

yond the text to decipher its meaning or possible meanings. Most critics agree with Richard Cary, who reads Sylvia's choice as a sign of Jewett's clear advocation of country values over city values, but there are some who view it as a sign of an exploration of sexual conflicts and social tensions, as an allegory of Jewett's own rejection of marriage and ultimately as evidence of her aversion to adulthood.[46] Renza interprets Sylvia's silence as an extension of the numerous rhetorical questions at the end of the story which summarily constitute Jewett's conscious and ironic withdrawal from those tropes that would define and consequently limit her work as minor or regional literature.[47] I tend to agree with Theodore Hovet that the story is a form of folk or fairy tale that Jewett uses to explore "the mythic roots of the conflicts generated by the encounter of modern social forces with provincial America."[48]

But I would go a step further by suggesting that she also explores the sexual conflict between feminine independence and masculine domination that recalls the abduction of Persephone. Sylvia essentially averts the fate of Persephone by her silence, and hence Jewett withdraws not only from tropes such as minor or regional literature but from patriarchal versions of folktales and fairy tales in which the male either bribes or rescues a female from an environment he deems less than desirable for her. "A White Heron," consequently, is a narrative inversion not only of the Persephone myth but of the Cinderella fairy tale.[49] Jewett uses this narrative inversion to call into question received cultural norms about country and city values and about masculine and feminine

46. Cary, "Introduction," in *Deephaven*, 21. For a discussion of Sylvia's decision to remain silent, also see Brenzo, "Free Heron"; Hovet, "Once Upon a Time"; Eugene Hillhouse Pool, "The Child in Sarah Orne Jewett," *Colby Library Quarterly*, VII (1967), 503–509; and Wood, "Literature of Impoverishment."
47. Renza, *"White Heron,"* 67–71, 86–94.
48. Hovet, "Once Upon a Time," 63.
49. Annis Pratt, "Women and Nature in Modern Fiction," *Contemporary Literature*, XIII (1972), 476–90. Donovan also discusses Cinderella motifs in Jewett in *New England Local Color Literature*, 107–10.

perspectives toward human experience. Implicit in her tale is the call to affirm and celebrate those values and perspectives that are customarily and often automatically minimized and to consider how American culture might be transformed.

Despite the triumphs of Sylvia's rite of passage, "A White Heron" remains a highly symbolic, almost metaphysical story. Consequently, Jewett's preoccupation with the need to know the world and the village and the city and the country appears in oblique terms.[50] In "The Flight of Betsey Lane" (1893) and "The Hiltons' Holiday" (1895) this preoccupation is more apparent, and it takes on less symbolic and more explicit, realistic hues. The journeys are therefore horizontal rather than vertical, emphasizing the complementary needs for self-affirmation and connection to others. Betsey Lane's journey to Philadelphia, for example, is inspired by a long-hoped-for opportunity to "see something of the world before she dies" (174). The By-Fleet Poor-House, where she resides, has ironic undertones of being both a prison and a haven. Its inhabitants, referred to as "inmates," do not lament their situation but actually like "the change and excitement" that their winter "residence" provides (172). Yet, as the youngest of the three spinster friends, Betsey Lane seeks greater excitement than the poorhouse offers. The opportunity to realize her dream comes in the form of one hundred dollars, a sum that furnishes her with a "sense of her own consequence" (179) reminiscent of the urgent "wish for wings" that Nina Auerbach contends is characteristic of the spinster as hero.[51] Thus we are prepared for the description of her disappearance as a discovery that she "had flown" (182) and for her departure to be termed a "flitting" (183) and an "escape" (185). In other worlds, flight has connotations of wish fulfillment, independent choice, unlimited potential, and birdlike freedom from captivity.

50. Willa Cather, *Not Under Forty* (New York, 1936), 83.

51. Auerbach, *Woman and the Demon*, 111–12. Also see Johns, "'Mateless and Appealing,'" 147–65.

The journey of her friends to search for her is termed a "fruit-less expedition" (192), but her journey is thoroughly productive. It provides her with much-desired escape from narrow circumstances, with knowledge of the world (almost literally, in that the centennial she attends is the equivalent of a world's fair), and with a sense of rejuvenation and fulfillment. Yet her return points to another way in which her excursion has been productive. When she informs her friends that she has brought each of them a "little somethin'" (192), her words signify more than the material tokens of friendship she gives them. These words also suggest the greater gifts of spiritual renewal she wishes to offer by sharing the story of her journey with them. The female hero's return is character-ized by an urgent desire to share and reaffirm communal ties that is almost as urgent as the previous desire to take flight. In sum, Betsey Lane's return has powers of transformation: it changes the three friends from mere bean-pickers into a "small elderly company . . . of triumphant" women (193). They become a "mi-raculous sisterhood" such as Nina Auerbach describes in *Communities of Women*.[52] Enriched vicariously by their friend's journey to the city and more specifically by the story of that journey, these women find it easier to endure the realities of their meager exis-tence in the country.

In "The Hiltons' Holiday" we have less a sense that the young Hilton girls, one of whom is nine years old, seek to escape their country farm than that their father seeks to give them a "treat" (292) away from it. Nevertheless, their excursion into town is an-other example of the value of the female journey for herself and her community. The girls' father suggests the excursion as an "opportunity to know the world" and "see how other folks do things" (292–93), while their mother advocates the virtues of the country and the comfort of home. Her less than enthusiastic re-sponse to the proposed trip is emphasized by her stasis in the

52. Nina Auerbach, *Communities of Women: An Idea in Fiction* (Cambridge, Mass., 1978), 10.

rocking chair and her questioning "why folks want . . . to go trapesin' off to strange places when such things is happenin' right about 'em" (294). The image of the mother in the rocking chair not only suggests the cyclic ritual of female time that Mircea Eliade calls the time of the "eternal return," but it also connects her to the place traditionally associated with a woman's sphere— the home.[53] Moreover, her words invoke Jewett's awareness of her native region's concomitant self-sufficiency and deprivation as it reluctantly faced late nineteenth-century changes in attitude toward country and city life. Her words questioning the value of a trip to town also echo Jewett's belief that a "dull little country village is just the place to find the real drama of life."[54]

The characterization of the Hilton girls illustrates how the journey can blur the stereotypical distinctions between town and country. Before the journey, the two sisters are shown representing the traditional dichotomy between the female who readily accepts the confines of hearth and home and the one who does not.[55] Susan Ellen is a "complete little housekeeper" (291), and Kathy ventures "out o'doors [to] hark . . . [to] bird[s]" (292), a description that recalls Sylvia in "A White Heron." Ironically, the "holiday" trip to town transforms the girls. When they return, their mother perceives that both "children looked different . . . as if they belonged to the town as much as to the country" (304). Their transformation suggests that a woman need not deny one to enjoy the other but that she could affirm both.

The journey as an excursion into the past, not the journey itself, changes them. Like the two visitors in *Deephaven,* whose

53. Donovan reviews Jewett's literary rubric in the context of recent feminist theories about female experience in "Jewett's Critical Theory," in *Critical Essays,* ed. Nagel, 218–19. See also Rabuzzi, *The Sacred and the Feminine,* 143–51; and Mircea Eliade, *The Myth of the Eternal Return* (Princeton, 1974), 153.

54. Jewett, "Preface to 1893 Edition," in *Deephaven and Other Stories,* ed. Cary, 31. The phrase about the "real drama of life" is quoted in Cary, "Introduction," *ibid.,* 9.

55. Donovan, *New England Local Color Literature,* 1–10.

journey is characterized by numerous narrative exchanges with people who share their individual and collective stories of village life, the Hilton girls' visit to town is characterized by opportunities to hear stories of their own family history. In addition, they listen to memories of the town's elderly, and they have their picture taken with their father. Thus, once again narrative in Jewett's fiction serves as a source of personal and shared history and as a form of communal affirmation. The journey into the past through storytelling is a valuable investment in the "riches of association and remembrance" (304) from which they would continually draw as they travel the road to self-knowledge.

In short, flight and return are not mutually exclusive experiences but are the affirmation of desire in Jewett's women. The circularity of the journey does not signify the impoverishment that Ann Douglas Wood and others have suggested;[56] instead, it signifies the ritualistic pattern of desire, expectation, fulfillment, and renewed desire that characterizes the cycle of human experience. Jewett illustrates that the desire that accompanies a female hero's return is not to subdue objects to her own purpose as a male hero does but to reconnect and share with the community from which she departed.[57] Accordingly, the Hilton girls, whose lives have been enriched by the day's excursion, return home to share their experiences with their mother, and in that way they enrich her life as well. The ultimate reward for the journey out is the opportunity for growth and fulfillment of desire; concurrently, the reward for the journey back is the reservoir of remembrance, self-discovery, and renewed desire. Neither journey precludes the significance of the other.

By using feminine rituals of flight and return in carefully devised circular narrative structures,[58] Jewett exposes the ironies that characterized the lives of many rural women in her time. On her own literary journey, she discovered that she need not be limited

56. Wood, "Literature of Impoverishment," 3–46.
57. Buchan, *Our Dear Sarah*, 45.
58. Ammons, "Going in Circles."

by the local-color medium; she could transform it through her essentially affirmative vision.[59] Indeed, she journeyed beyond the artistic confines of local color into the comprehensive landscape we associate with myth.

59. Renza, *"White Heron,"* 169–78.

2

THE FICTIVE FENCE: THE COMPLEX RESPONSE TO LOSS IN *THE COUNTRY OF THE POINTED FIRS*

> People do not know what they lose when they make away with the reserve, the separateness, the sanctity of the front yard of their grandmothers. . . . We Americans had better build more fences than take away from our lives.
> —Sarah Orne Jewett, "From a Mournful Village"

> Good literature . . . is rooted in the invisible roots, the profoundest meanings of that place, race, or nationality; and to absorb and again effuse it, uttering words and products as from its midst, and carrying it into its highest regions is the work, or a main part of the work, of any country's true author.
> —Walt Whitman, "Democratic Vistas"

Sarah Orne Jewett's fiction exhibits her intimate concern with loss.[1] This loss often appears in personal and situational forms, but Jewett also leads her reader to consider loss in a larger cultural and historical context. She invites her reader to contemplate the past and to consider what might be retrieved, reclaimed, and affirmed by being integrated into the present. Nowhere is this profound sense of loss and preoccupation with the past more clearly expressed than in *The Country of the Pointed Firs* (1896). In this work Jewett consciously retrieves the "invisible roots" associated with her native Maine that she evoked in the writing of *Deephaven* nineteen years earlier. While reclaiming these roots, her fictional

---

1. Martin, *Harvests of Change*, 43. Martin uses the term *fictive fence* to describe Jewett's means of preserving the "flourishing past of her birthplace, South Berwick, Maine." I have appropriated the term not only to describe Jewett's narrative intent but to signify her literary aesthetic and to identify an important feature of her narrative strategy.

narratives betray the possibility that they do not need to be re-claimed at all but are still very much a part of the present she sought to describe in following her father's advice to "tell things just as they are."[2] Thus her descriptions of New England people and places suggest that the roots of the past need not be retrieved but acknowledged and affirmed in the interest of transforming the cultural attitudes of the American consciousness.

Essentially, the narrative technique in *Pointed Firs* is at once a "strategy of containment"—the construction of a "fictive fence"—to preserve folk roots, and a vehicle for critiquing those cultural and historical forces that would preclude Jewett from making these roots the stuff of literature or that would preclude her from taking these materials to the "highest regions" of myth.[3] This nar-rative technique encodes Jewett's problematic desire to save a van-ishing way of life by inscribing it in fiction. But the irony of her desire lies in the contradictory implications of her literary project, for at the same time that she seeks to affirm her rural cultural roots, she unwittingly perpetuates their marginal status by en-closing them. Her novel thus raises the question whether it is pos-sible for a woman writer to affirm hidden values, to make them more visible and accessible, without reifying the forces of cultural domination that threaten her feminist vision. Or as Sarah Sher-man argues, the woman writer inevitably confronts the "paradox of the marginal center . . . crucial to the consciousness of any person not identified with cultural authority."[4] The complexity of Jewett's literary response to this question and to the question of loss in *Pointed Firs* can be appreciated only when her folk aesthetic

2. Cary, ed., *Jewett Letters*, 52.

3. Fredric Jameson, *The Political Unconscious: Narrative as a Socially Symbolic Act* (Ithaca, 1981), 53. The term *strategy of containment* is borrowed from Jameson to refer to intellectual and formal constructs of ideological limits. This strategy is related to Louis Renza's argument that Jewett consciously attempts to write minor literature. I believe her aim is not to write minor literature but to appropriate these materials (especially myth) associated with major literature both to subvert that literature and to claim a place in it.

4. Sherman, *Sarah Orne Jewett*, 5.

and mythic impulse are viewed as signs of her revisionist attitude toward late nineteenth-century America. Jewett's response to loss must be examined to determine how the text signifies on the past from the narrator's point of view, how the narrator's understanding of the past changes and transforms her consciousness, and how the text ultimately challenges cultural, sexual, and even literary norms.[5]

The situation of the narrator in *Pointed Firs* is established by the words *the return,* the very first words of the text and the title of the first chapter. Described as a "lover of Dunnet Landing" (13), the narrator reveals that this is not her first visit but a return visit after two or three summers. As the novel begins, she has "returned to find the unchanged shores of the pointed firs, the same quaintness of the village with its elaborate conventionalities, all that mixture of remoteness and childish certainty of being the center of civilization of which her affectionate dreams had told" (13). Inherent in this description of Dunnet Landing is the influence of the interplay of memory and desire on the perspective the narrator brings to the landscape on her return visit. The narrator is remembering a place and desiring that it be exactly as she remembered it. It is perhaps the confluence of memory and desire that accounts for the almost excessive comparison through qualification and simile that characterizes the first paragraph of the novel:

There was something about the coast town of Dunnet which made it *seem more* attractive than other maritime villages of eastern Maine.

5. I am not the first to recognize Jewett's preoccupation with the past. Typically, critics view her attitude toward the past in terms of ambivalence, naive nostalgia, and escapism through the pastoral. Though there are resonances of each of these, none of them fully accounts for Jewett's treatment of the past. It seems to me that she does not so much retreat to the past as attempt to revise cultural values of her own time by infusing them with the essential elements of a devalued past. Some of the best critical assessments of her use of the past include Berthoff, "Jewett's *Pointed Firs*"; Ferman Bishop, "The Sense of the Past in Sarah Orne Jewett," in *Appreciation of Sarah Orne Jewett,* ed. Cary, 135–43; Martin, *Harvests of Change;* and Stevenson, "Double Consciousness."

Perhaps it was the simple fact of acquaintance with that neighborhood which made it so attaching and gave such interest to the rocky shore and dark woods, and a few houses which *seemed* to be securely wedged and tree-nailed in among the ledges of the Landing. These houses made the most of their seaward view, and there was gayety and determined floweriness in their bits of garden ground; the small-paned high windows in the peaks of their steep gables were *like* knowing eyes that watched the harbor and the far sea-line beyond, or looked northward all along the shore and its background of spruces and balsam firs. When one really knows a village like this and its surroundings, it is *like* becoming acquainted with a single person. The process of falling in love at first sight is as final as it is swift in such a case, but the growth of true friendship may be a lifelong affair. (13; emphasis added).

The comparisons in this passage not only suggest the means by which the narrator connects memory and desire, but they also foreshadow portraits of the people who inhabit this landscape by encoding descriptions of the people within descriptions of their homes. An example of this descriptive encoding is the phrase *securely wedged,* which describes the few houses of Dunnet Landing that are among the ledges. Beneath the oxymoronic connotations of stability and restricted space associated with the houses is the paradoxical comfort and confinement associated with the lives of the village inhabitants. Similarly, the phrase *gayety and determined floweriness* not only signifies "bits of garden ground," but it also signifies rural women such as Mrs. Todd, who possess a resplendent determination to make "the most of [their] seaward view" and restricted circumstances. Paradoxical descriptions such as these not only foreshadow the narrative tension that runs throughout *Pointed Firs,* but they also account for why many Jewett scholars see ambivalence as the dominant tone of her fiction.[6] Although it is tempting to read this narrative tension as

6. See Stevenson, "Double Consciousness," 1–3; and Berthoff, "Jewett's *Pointed Firs,*" 52.

ambivalence, in light of the cultural affirmation that pervades the text the more cogent argument is that these descriptions signify the strength and vitality of this landscape despite the forces around it that would weaken or destroy it.

Ironically, in associating her knowledge of the village with becoming acquainted with a single person, the narrator reveals that another form of revision is also the subject of her narrative. Not only does she return to look again at this place that has inhabited her memory and desires, but in the process of looking again, she moves beyond re-vision as looking back to revision as a retrospective process that leads to transformation and growth, a process similar to what Adrienne Rich describes as entering an old text from a new critical direction.[7] In this process, the landscape becomes a text to be reread and measured against memory and desire. As a reader and rereader of this regional landscape, the narrator tells her own version of its story as she simultaneously interprets the stories she receives from those who inhabit the landscape. Annette Kolodny reminds us that "interpretive strategies . . . are learned, historically determined and thereby necessarily gender-inflected."[8] If we apply this idea to the situation in *Pointed Firs,* we see the narrator's return to Dunnet Landing as more than a second summer visit. Instead, it is an opportunity to shed a male interpretive strategy that would marginalize the region and its people. It is a journey back in time and space that would alter her consciousness and permit her to grow beyond "love at first sight" into a more profound appreciation of the landscape. The result of this "revisionary" process is the kind of problematic narrative that Brooks associates with psychoanalysis in which "the reader [in this case, the narrator] is called upon to participate in the telling and the completion of the narrative in

7. Adrienne Rich, "When We Dead Awaken: Writing as Re-Vision," *College English,* XXXIV (October, 1972), 18.
8. Annette Kolodny, "A Map for Rereading; or, Gender and the Interpretation of Literary Texts," *New Literary History,* II (1980), 452–53.

order to make it fully hermeneutic."[9] *Pointed Firs,* therefore, is ultimately a narrative reconstruction of this second visit, a reconstruction of the past that forsakes naive nostalgia and learned condescension to incorporate overlooked and essentially female regional realities into a more mature, empathetic perspective.

But the word *return* is full of other resonances that figure into our interpretation of this text. Although it ostensibly signifies a response to loss that involves the narrator's conscious desire to connect a remembered time and place from the past with the present moment, it also signifies a revision of literary convention, it evokes the image of "home," and it alludes to the cyclical realm of time we associate with myth and ritual. Because the novel begins with a return and ends with a departure, it offers an immediate revision of the male linear plot in which the departure is the beginning and the return is the end. Instead, it revises this literary convention in accordance with a feminine mode of ordering experience.[10] This mode of ordering experience is weblike, nuclear rather than linear, moving back and forth from a nexus of nature and nurturance. It integrates a perspective toward the past that seems ahistorical one moment ("unchanged shores of the pointed firs") and intrinsically historical the next ("the centre of civilization"). Indeed, Jewett's inversion of the traditional plot structure reminds us of T. S. Eliot's response to the past in "Four Quartets" in which "what we call the beginning is often the end / And to make an end is to make a beginning. / The end is where we start from."[11] Thus Jewett's literary revision, signaled by the word *return,* suggests that an appreciation of the value and significance of this regional space and earlier time rests on a willingness to return to it and see it from a new perspective. In fact, as suggested in the

9. Brooks, *Reading for the Plot,* 320–21. I borrow my use of the term *revisionary* from Kolodny, "Map for Rereading," 465.

10. See Ammons, "Going in Circles"; Donovan, "Jewett's Critical Theory," 218–19; and Rabuzzi, *The Sacred and the Feminine,* 143–53.

11. T. S. Eliot, "Four Quartets," in *Collected Poems, 1909–1962* (New York, 1963), 207.

previous chapter, the notion of return is part of the cyclical paradigm that determines the narrative structure of much of Jewett's
fiction, but especially *Pointed Firs*.

The word *return* also invokes the image of home. Drawing on
the memories of her own literal home, Jewett portrays a narrator
who seeks to return to a figurative home, a haven away from the
urban milieu of Boston. Dunnet Landing thus becomes "the reserve, the separateness, [and] sanctity of the front yard of . . .
grandmothers" that Jewett seeks to preserve in fiction. It is therefore fitting that the narrator begin her story here, especially if we
accept Eliot's dictum that "home is where we start from."[12] Words
and phrases such as *attaching, securely, knowing eyes, love, childish
certainty of being the centre*, and *affectionate* all suggest that the narrator is not simply a visitor but a kind of prodigal daughter of this
rural "rooted" landscape.[13] Yet even as the narrator expresses her
affection for this landscape, she acknowledges the sense of remoteness that seems to undermine her attachment. Words such as
far sea line and *quaint* point to the physical and emotional distance
between this rural home and the urban one from which she has
fled. As the novel progresses, however, this distance is mitigated
by the narrator's growing awareness of how the folk of this region
are connected to an even more remote time—that of the mythic
past. Indeed, what enriches the text of *Pointed Firs* is the way the
mythic implications of return not only enlarge the significance of
the narrator's visit but posit her narrative in the complex network
of meaning found in the cyclical time of ritual.[14] Consequently,
the mythic resonances of return reaffirm the narrator's attachment
to this landscape.

Yet the transformation that the narrator undergoes does not

12. *Ibid.*, 189.

13. Julia Bader, "The 'Rooted' Landscape and the Woman Writer," in *Teaching
Women's Literature from a Regional Perspective*, ed. Lenore Hoffman and Deborah
Rosenfelt (New York, 1982), 23.

14. Raphael Patai, *Myth and Modern Man* (Englewood Cliffs, N.J., 1972), 3.
Also see Eliade, *Myth of the Eternal Return*, 141–47.

rest on her attachment to the landscape per se. It rests more specifically on the relationships she develops with the people of
Dunnet Landing as she observes them, listens to their stories, and
participates with them in the rituals of their community. At the
center of this community is Mrs. Almira Todd, the narrator's
landlady and guide into the interior of this community. It is the
"deeper intimacy" (16) that develops between them that sets the
process of revision and transformation in motion. Through Mrs.
Todd, the narrator begins to recognize those aspects of the folk
and mythic past that are alive in the present and that sustained
this rural community in the past. She begins to realize how this
past is lost only to those who do not respect it and to those who
have not ventured to understand it. Thus the characterization of
Mrs. Todd most clearly exemplifies the folk aesthetic and mythic
impulse at work in Jewett's fiction.

Until recently, the term *local color* has been considered so pe-
jorative that the folk aesthetic embedded within much regionalist
fiction has either been taken for granted or ignored altogether.[15]
Consequently, most discussions of Mrs. Todd simply acknowledge the description of her as an herbal priestess and move on to
focus on the mythic implications of her characterization. By examining the folk dimensions of her character, however, we can
begin to understand that folk materials in *Pointed Firs* do not
merely "decorate" the text in the interest of realism; instead, they
deepen the depiction of characters like Mrs. Todd, and they com-
plement Jewett's serious aesthetic and narrative intentions.[16]

The entire second chapter is devoted to introducing Mrs. Todd,
a woman described as an "ardent lover of herbs" and "a very large

15. Glenda Hobbs, "Harriet Arnow's Kentucky Novels: Beyond Local Color,"
in *Regionalism and the Female Imagination: A Collection of Essays,* ed. Emily Toth
(New York, 1985), 83–85.

16. Pry, "Folk-Literary Aesthetics," 7. Very little critical attention has been
devoted to the folk dimensions of Jewett's fiction. Noteworthy exceptions, besides
Pry, are Perry D. Westbrook, *The New England Town in Fact and Fiction* (Madison,
N.J., 1982); Susan Joan Martin Fagan, "Sarah Orne Jewett's Fiction: A Reevaluation from Three Perspectives," *Dissertation Abstracts International,* XLIII (August,
1982), 445A; and Ammons, "Jewett's Witches."

person" (14). The first description points to her folk occupation, the second to the larger-than-life dimensions of her character that the narrator later apprehends in mythic terms. In fact, the entire portrait of Mrs. Todd is delineated by a balanced presentation of folk and mythic characteristics, as exemplified in the narrator's description of the "rustic pharmacopea" found in her herb garden: "There were some strange and pungent odors that roused a dim sense and remembrance of something in the forgotten past. Some of these might once have belonged to sacred and mystic rites, and have had some occult knowledge handed with them down the centuries; but now they pertained only to humble compounds brewed at intervals with molasses or vinegar or spirits in a small cauldron on Mrs. Todd's kitchen stove. They were dispensed to suffering neighbors, who usually came at night as if by stealth, bringing their own ancient-looking vials to be filled" (14).

This description deepens the portrait of Mrs. Todd in three respects: it implicitly associates her, through her garden, with a forgotten past; it links her folk practices to magic and the supernatural; and it connects her, through folk medicine, with the people of her community. These interconnections between the past, magic, and the community appear again at the end of the second chapter, where the narrator observes: "She stood in the centre of a braided rug, and its rings of black and gray seemed to circle about her feet in the dim light. Her height and massiveness in the low room gave her the look of a huge sibyl, while the strange fragrance of the mysterious herb blew in from the little garden" (17). Here Mrs. Todd is not only connected to the occult, but, as the image of a "sibyl" signifies, she is also connected to the ancient Greek female oracular or prophetess figure. Indeed, Jewett inverts the negative stereotype of a witch as an evil, deviant woman into a positive one of a female hero whose attributes of nurturance and wisdom help sustain others.[17] By so doing, she subverts the male patriarchal norm that would make Mrs. Todd a

17. See Ammons, "Jewett's Witches."

sinister figure and instead endows her with the benign image of folk healer and "rustic philosopher" (35)—an image that celebrates the feminine power of a conjure woman.

More than any other character, Mrs. Todd embodies the sense of the past that most essentially corresponds with the values Jewett seeks to affirm. She captures, in several ways, the spirit of the New England past associated with a preindustrial era. Unlike many of the other elderly denizens, who no longer feel needed or connected, at the age of sixty-seven she plays a vital, integral role in the lives of her neighbors, thereby affirming the communal interdependence of an earlier time. She is directly connected to the land through her livelihood as an herbalist and thus affirms the independence and resourcefulness of an agrarian past. Although others, especially men, have been occupationally displaced from the land, Mrs. Todd, with her folk practice, thrives on it.

As the narrator continues to observe this "landlady, herb gatherer and rustic philosopher" (35), she realizes that Mrs. Todd not only dispenses old-fashioned remedies to her neighbors but also accommodates their need to combine the "satisfaction of a friendly gossip with the medical opportunity" (18). Hence visits to her home become occasions to participate in the oral traditions that sustain the community. Likewise, Mrs. Todd not only treats physical ailments, but she also ministers to her neighbors' emotional concerns of "love and hate and jealousy and adverse winds at sea" (15). Thus she is the village healer and "oracle" (78) rolled into one.

Ironically, the fact that Dunnet Landing also has a regular doctor poses no threat for Mrs. Todd or the community. Rather than adversaries, the narrator tells us that they "were upon the best of terms" (15). On one hand, this complementary relationship might suggest that the two healers are of equal rank in the community. On the other, because Jewett dismisses the doctor with one short paragraph, it seems more likely that the value of the herbalist both encompasses and surpasses that of her male counterpart. The reader is reminded of the image of doctors that Jewett portrays in

her first novel, *A Country Doctor* (1884), just twelve years before
the publication of *Pointed Firs*. The protagonist, Nan Prince, realizes once she becomes a doctor that "beside medicines and ban-
dages and lessons in general hygiene for the physical ails of her
patients, she could often be a tonic to the mind and soul. . . .
Nobody sees people as they are and finds the chance to help poor
humanity as a doctor does. . . . The secrets of many hearts and
homes must be told to this confessor, and sadder ailments than
the text-books name are brought to be healed. . . . Teachers of
truth and givers of the laws of life, priests and ministers,—all
these professions are joined in one with the gift of healing."[18] Because Nan Prince appropriates a male tradition in becoming a doctor, she seems to foreshadow the later image of Mrs. Todd. Both
women view healing as a holistic process in which the strict science of medicine has only a minimal role. Thus Jewett's image of
Mrs. Todd again challenges a male norm and offers a revised perspective that is essentially feminine. I maintain that this is a conscious attempt despite Jewett's claim that her desire to rectify the
fictional image of the caricatured Yankee was unconscious. When
writing the 1893 Preface she was a seasoned author trying to account for her earlier narrative perspective in a literary climate that
she feared was not totally supportive of that perspective.

The simultaneous presence in Dunnet Landing of a medical
doctor and an herbalist also suggests that the past and present need
not conflict with each other. The auxiliary relationship between
the doctor and Mrs. Todd reveals that aspects of the past survive
in the present and contribute to the well-being of the community
as a whole. Thus, though there is some value in the authority of
modern science upon which the doctor's knowledge and authority
are based, there is equal if not greater value in the authority of
shared narratives in which women exchange "their own store of
therapeutic learning" (18). The narrator learns that it is in this
"school" that Mrs. Todd has strengthened her "natural gift" (18)

18. Sarah Orne Jewett, *A Country Doctor* (Boston, 1884), 342.

as a healer. That the reader is to assign greater value to the herb-alist's authority is clear when Mrs. Todd observes: "He's got too many long routes now to stop to tend to all his door patients . . . especially them that takes pleasure in talkin' themselves over. The doctor and me have got to be kind of partners; he's gone a good deal, far an' wide" (81). No doubt, this image of a doctor whose rounds curtail the quantity of time he could devote to his patients is partially drawn from Jewett's own childhood. She used to ac-company her physician father on his rounds along the country roads of Maine and certainly drew on these memories in her fic-tion.[19] Yet the positive nature of their relationship and the utmost respect she had for her father's profession appear to have been overshadowed by a growing fear that a former way of life was being threatened. Indeed, Mrs. Todd is a response to Jewett's fear that a rich cultural heritage connecting women and healing was about to be lost in the name of medical progress. Thus her portrait of this herbal priestess expresses both a tribute to a past female tradition and a hope that the tendency to marginalize and devalue that tradition could be reversed.

A very strong sense of the past emerges in the healing practices Mrs. Todd keeps alive. Not only is she linked to archaic traditions of medieval "witches" who used their semimagical knowledge of herbs and plants to treat their peasant clientele, but she is also linked to the tradition of lay medicine practiced by many women during American colonial times.[20] As a nineteenth-century herbal-ist, Mrs. Todd brings a professional air of confidence to this tra-dition in her assertion, "There's some herb that's good for every-

19. For discussions of Jewett's father, Dr. Theodore H. Jewett, see Fields, ed. *Letters of Jewett*, 4–5; Jewett, *Deephaven*, 7–8; and Matthiessen, *Jewett*, 12–14, 30.

20. Bair, "'Ties of Blood,'" 96–148. Bair discusses colonial patterns of care-taking that prevailed in the late nineteenth century. For discussions of references to herbal medicine in *Pointed Firs*, see Sylvia Gray Noyes, "Mrs. Almira Todd, Herbalist-Conjurer," *Colby Library Quarterly*, IX (1972), 643–49. An excellent source on the uses of some of the herbs mentioned in the text is Emrika Padus, *Woman's Encyclopedia of Health and Natural Healing* (Emmaus, Pa., 1981).

body except for them that thinks they're sick when they ain't" (51). But of all the herbs and plants associated with her—"hy'sop" (18), "tansy" (19), "bloodroot" (20), "simple" (20), and "camomile" (34)—"her favorite pennyroyal" (159) is perhaps the most significant. A stimulant aromatic used in the standard birthing tea to induce childbirth, pennyroyal has spiritual rather than physical powers in the context of this primarily elderly community of women.[21] Because its poignant aroma reminds Mrs. Todd of her deceased husband, Nathan, it has the power of recall. And in that this memory inspires her to share the story of her marriage, a story she seldom tells to anyone, pennyroyal gives birth to the deeper intimacy that develops between the narrator and Mrs. Todd. Thus the folk tradition of plant lore gives birth to the past, which gives birth to narrative, which in turn transforms the urban narrator's perspective toward and relationship with this rural herbalist and conjure woman.

But Mrs. Todd becomes part of the fictive fence Jewett uses to preserve the past in a more profound sense. At the same time that her folk traditions of self-reliant resourcefulness challenge male notions of modern scientific progress, they also recall the "archetypal figure long buried in women's collective memory [of] the earth goddess."[22] Thus, as an herbalist, Mrs. Todd is linked to the mythic past that connects women and nature. In her early observations of Mrs. Todd, the narrator does not recognize the mythic implications of this connection: "If Mrs. Todd had occasions to step into the far corner of her herb plot, she trod heavily upon thyme, and made its fragrant presence known with all the rest. Being a large person her full skirts brushed and bent almost every slender stalk that her feet missed. You could always tell when she was stepping about" (14). In that her presence seems to defy those forces that would marginalize her as an anachronism of a forgot-

21. See Noyes, "Mrs. Almira Todd," 647; Ammons, "Jewett's Witches," 175; and Padus, *Woman's Encyclopedia*, 305.
22. Pratt, *Archetypal Patterns*, 122–38.

ten past, the pun on "thyme" seems apt. Moreover, beyond this defiance is the affirmation of difference.

Although the sketch "The Queen's Twin" was added to *Pointed Firs* posthumously by Willa Cather, the narrator's observation of Mrs. Todd in this sketch not only echoes the earlier description but reveals the narrator's recognition of the mythic dimensions inherent in Mrs. Todd's character:[23] "Life was very strong in her, as if some force of Nature were personified in this simplehearted woman and gave her cousinship to the ancient deities. She might have walked the primeval fields of Sicily; her strong gingham skirts might at that very moment bend the slender stalks of asphodel and be fragrant with trodden thyme, instead of the brown wind-brushed goldenrod" (137). Again, there is an apparent pun on the word *thyme,* but whereas it was in the process of being trod upon in the former passage, it is already trodden down in the latter. Thus the narrator's perception of Mrs. Todd's relationship to time (or the past) is colored by the present moment in the first description, but in the second, she realizes that Mrs. Todd is strongly connected to a more ancient time. Read another way, we could interpret both passages as versions of a disregard for time that affirms the authority and transcendent power of a devalued self. Regardless of the interpretation, the narrator's second description clearly acknowledges the signs of the mythic past that infuse Mrs. Todd's character with larger-than-life significance. By recognizing the mythic narrative that is part of Mrs. Todd's story, the narrator revises her view of her as a quaint old woman and begins to perceive the heroic qualities derived from the folk and mythic roots that have shaped her.

One of these heroic qualities is self-sufficiency, which is appar-

23. In her edition of *Pointed Firs,* Marjorie Pryse mentions the reordering of chapters that Cather did at the prompting of a publisher. The three stories added, known as the Dunnet Landing Sketches, are "A Dunnet Shepherdess," "The Queen's Twin," and "William's Wedding." See Marjorie Pryse, "Introduction to the Norton Edition," in Sarah Orne Jewett, *The Country of the Pointed Firs* (New York, 1981), v–xx.

ent both in the self-reliance by which Mrs. Todd supports herself and in her relationships with others. For example, when the narrator asks about getting a man to help them take a large boat to Green Island, Mrs. Todd assures her that they can "man" a dory themselves. She adds, "We don't want to carry no men folks havin' to be considered every minute an' takin' up all our time" (35). This seemingly minor decision not only demonstrates her self-reliance, but it suggests the social changes villages such as Dunnet Landing have undergone. Whereas in the seafaring past, women relied on men, *Pointed Firs* focuses on a time when the vagaries of technological progress spelled the end of the shipping industry and compelled men to relinquish their dominant status. The status of men is thus transferred to or, more accurately, appropriated by women like Mrs. Todd, who prove themselves more resilient in the face of economic transition. But as Donovan and other critics assert, this appropriation of status is really a re-appropriation or a return of women to their former matriarchal status in a time when women depended on one another.[24] Nevertheless, the narrator's question clearly inserts into the text the traditional perspective toward male and female roles, a perspective consistent with urban values outside of rural places like Dunnet Landing. In this instance, therefore, Jewett's response to the past is a challenge to Victorian cultural and sexual norms, and it is an affirmation of an older tradition of feminine self-reliance and interdependence.

Jewett's response to the past in *Pointed Firs* is further enriched by her conscious appropriation of women's mythic roots—namely, the narrative of Demeter and Persephone—to portray the relationship between Mrs. Todd and the narrator. This mythic narrative connects the bond between the young urban visitor and her older rural guide to an ancient mother-daughter relationship, recalls a tradition of feminine triumph over adversity and male

24. See Sherman, "Victorians and the Matriarchal Mythology"; Donovan, *New England Local Color Literature,* 117–18; and Auerbach, *Communities of Women.*

control, and affirms patterns of transformation and regeneration in nature that parallel female experience.[25] Although the growth of the relationship between the narrator and Mrs. Todd forms the basic plot of the novel, always present below the surface of the text is the conflict between the urban and rural environments associated with each woman. Usually this conflict ruptures the surface of the text in the narratives of the villagers, but occasionally it appears in the narrator's comments. When it does, it offers a possible explanation for her desire to flee the city and return to Dunnet Landing. Her reflection on city life in Chapter 23, "William's Wedding," suggests how the urban milieu assaults her spirit and inspires her flight to the country:

> The hurry of life in a large town, the constant putting aside of preference to yield to a most unsatisfactory activity, began to vex me, and one day I took the train, and only left it for the eastward-bound boat. . . . The complexity and futile ingenuity of social life seems a conspiracy. But the first salt wind from the east . . . the flash of a gull, the waiting procession of seaward-bound firs on an island, made me feel solid and definite again, instead of a poor, incoherent being. Life was resumed, and anxious living blew away as if it had not been. I could not breathe deep enough or long enough. It was a return to happiness. (147)

If we view the city life from which the narrator has fled as a kind of underworld for the dead, where the forces of the male patriarchy commit spiritual rape, then the narrator's return to the country is akin to Persephone's return from Hades. Mrs. Todd thus becomes Demeter, whose mourning for her daughter's rape and traumatic abduction ends upon her annual return to earth.

25. See Sherman, "Victorians and the Matriarchal Mythology," 63–74, and Sherman, *Sarah Orne Jewett*, 91–117, for discussions of how the Demeter-Persephone myth is configured in the characterization of Mrs. Todd and the narrator. Also see Pratt, *Archetypal Patterns*, 170–78; and Pratt, "Woman and Nature."

In that the narrator's return is also a journey into an Eden that has suffered yet survived the pains of "progress," it provides an opportunity to experience renewal through communion with her spiritual mother and guide. The trip to Green Island to visit Mrs. Blackett, the mother of Mrs. Todd, sharpens the narrator's sense of that setting as a female sanctuary from the encroachment of male control, a setting Donovan refers to as a "world of mothers."[26] Thus the narrator's journey, which she likens to a "spell" (34), transforms her from a stranger into an "adopted" (89) daughter of an "enchantress" (34). Moreover, the Demeter-Persephone connection is deepened by the portrait of Mrs. Todd as an herbalist or earth mother whose livelihood directly connects her to vegetation cycles of growth, death, harvest, and renewal that mirror female reproductive cycles. By drawing on these mythic roots, Jewett preserves and affirms one way of life as she offers a critique of another.

The final sense in which Mrs. Todd epitomizes the past is in her knowledge of the history of Dunnet Landing. Much of what the narrator learns about this region comes either directly or indirectly from Mrs. Todd, who possesses a "natural gift" for story-telling. When a neighbor dies, it is Mrs. Todd who tells "all [the] neighbor's history" (20). When they go to visit Mrs. Todd's brother William, it is Mrs. Todd who "told all the news there was to tell" (46). The narrator observes, furthermore, that Mrs. Todd was "usually unerring in matters of genealogy" (83), and she possessed a "peculiar wisdom that made one value [her] . . . pleasant company" (84). Not only is she a griot or oral historian, who, through "constant interest and intercourse . . . link[s] the far island . . . and scattered farms into a golden chain of love and independence" (82), but she is also a kind of archivist whose speech reveals a collection of proverbial sayings and expressions. For example, of two farmers who have become enemies, she explains: "Each of 'em tells the neighbors their wrongs; plenty likes

26. Donovan, *New England Local Color Literature,* 99–118.

to hear and tell again; them as fetch a bone'll carry one, an' so they keep the fight a-goin'" (37). Of herself, she asserts: "I must say I like variety myself; some folks washes Monday an' irons Tuesday the whole year round, even if the circus is goin' by" (37). On friendship, she comments: "Yes'm old friends is always best, 'less you catch a new one that's fit to make an old one out of" (58). Elmer Pry notes that these expressions are not mere local color but signs of the collective wisdom of the community and Mrs. Todd's own authority and folk erudition.[27] Because she knows the genealogy and history of the village, and because she is intimately and intricately woven into the lives of the people through the oral tradition and folk healing, Mrs. Todd *is* the past.

For the narrator, she "loomed large" (41). As the village spokeswoman, she is both the narrator's guide into the community and her interpreter of its past. As Mrs. Todd's friend Mrs. Fosdick asserts: "I see so many of these new folks nowadays, that seem to have neither past nor future. Conversation's got to have some root in the past, or else you've got to explain every remark you make, an' it wears a person out" (58). Clearly, Mrs. Todd is a root of the folk past. She is also a root of the mythic past. At the point that the narrator recognizes the dual roots of this griot figure, she makes an existential leap to suggest that even in her simplicity, Mrs. Todd has a grandeur and complexity the narrator had not expected: "There was something lonely and solitary about her great-determined shape. She might have been Antigone alone on the Theban plain. . . . An absolute, archaic grief possessed this countrywoman; she seemed like a renewal of some historic soul, with her sorrows and the remoteness of a daily life busied with rustic simplicities and the scents of primeval herbs" (49).

This comparison comes immediately after Mrs. Todd confides cherished memories of her deceased husband. If we recall that Antigone defied the authority of the patriarchy, the comparison could be interpreted to suggest Mrs. Todd's defiance of a prevail-

27. Pry, "Folk-Literary Aesthetics," 9.

ing selfishness she observed in which "there's more women likes to be loved than there is of those that loves" (49). The relationship she reminisces about is one of friendship in marriage rather than one in which the husband was a mere caretaker. The passage could also be interpreted as a comparison of women mourning the loss of innocence to patriarchal violation or material gain. Yet it might also refer to Jewett's implicit defiance of a literary authority that would trivialize or marginalize the grief of a country woman. Jewett thus appropriates a male literary tradition—Greek myth—and uses it to challenge and ultimately subvert that tradition in the interest of reclaiming and revising feminine power.[28] Thus the allusion to Greek myth suggests a quality in Mrs. Todd that transcends her own particular place and time but does not negate it. Because her wisdom and knowledge are an "intimation of truth itself," the narrator realizes that Mrs. Todd "might belong to any age, like an idyll of Theocritus" (56). With this recognition, the narrator reveals that her own understanding of Mrs. Todd has been transformed. She is not as quaint or strange or even mystical as she once seemed. Instead, like Mrs. Blackett, she merely seems "to keep the balance true, and make up to all her scattered and depending neighbors for other things which they may have lacked" (47).

If Mrs. Todd represents balance, then two other village denizens, Captain Littlepage and Joanna Todd, represent the loss or lack of balance. Both characters are denizens only in the way their life stories make up the larger story of the village. Actually both live in a self-imposed exile, although Captain Littlepage's exile is mental and Joanna's is physical and spiritual. Both are examples of the conflict between old and new values, past and present time, and rural and urban life that occasionally ruptures the texture of this affirmative female landscape. The stories of Captain Littlepage and Joanna are nevertheless part of the complex response to

28. Renza, *"White Heron,"* 196, refers to Greek myth as a patriarchal tradition that Jewett calls into question.

loss that Jewett seeks to weave into the text. Their stories intimate much about the forces of change that have altered the region. Together their stories provide the narrator with another vision/ version of this place and of the past. Yet the rupture they create in the texture of the narrative is not accidental on Jewett's part. Rather, it is consistent with her desire to portray the truth and complexity of country life. Thus the stories of Captain Littlepage and Joanna do not negate this desire as much as they sharpen the truth and complexity she seeks to inscribe within her realistic rendering of this time and place.

The narrator initially learns very little about Captain Littlepage from Mrs. Todd, who protectively "seemed to class him with her other secrets." The narrator is thus led to regard him as one who "might have belonged with a simple which grew in a certain slug-haunted corner of the garden, whose use she [Mrs. Todd] could never be betrayed into telling" (20). The narrator first sees him in Mrs. Todd's garden; thus it is apt that she first notices how the "simple" and "slug-haunted corner" mirror the only two pieces of information she knows about him: that he had "overset his mind with too much reading" and that he occasionally had "spells of some unexplainable nature" (22). It is only when the captain pays a surprise visit to the narrator that she learns his own personal story as well as his version of the story of the region.

Captain Littlepage is a former seaman who is doomed to dreaming of and lamenting his past life. Though he admits "it was a dog's life," he nevertheless feels "it made men of those who followed it" (25). The loss of this way of life both saddens and embitters him. Moreover, his displacement from the sea leaves him completely out of touch with, yet profoundly aware of, the reality of his life. His hallucinations about a mysterious town where a captain and his crew are held captive in a "kind of waiting-place between this world an' the next" (30) signify his flight from reality into the extreme interior of his imagination. The notion of a midworld accurately describes what Dunnet Landing has become for men like the captain who are wedged in

time between memories of a glorious past and visions of a hope-
less future. Unfortunately, some critics have construed his tragic,
pessimistic perspective as a sign of Jewett's own descent into "historical petrification."[29] Such an interpretation, however, misreads
what the captain's narrative adds to the text. It also misreads
Jewett's aesthetic intention and narrative strategy. The fictive fence
she constructs could not reject the narrative of one whose fate was
in many ways connected to and indicative of the fate of the entire
region.

The demoralized captain's only solace comes from reciting
Shakespeare, reading Milton's *Paradise Lost,* and sharing stories of
his former seafaring days. Yet his rambling narratives reveal more
than his own personal fate of "having to suffer at the hands of the
ignorant" (24). The "change for the worse" (25) that he tells of
refers not so much to his own situation as to the loss of an entire
way of life. Indeed, it is Captain Littlepage who most clearly articulates how the vast historical and economic changes that took
place in the early nineteenth century altered the social and cultural
makeup of this regional landscape:

> A community narrows down and grows dreadful ignorant when it is
> shut up to its own affairs, and gets no knowledge of the outside world
> except from a cheap, unprincipled newspaper. In the old days, a good
> part o' the best men here knew a hundred ports and something of the
> way folks lived in them. They saw the world for themselves, and like's
> not their wives and children saw it with them. They may not have had
> the best of knowledge to carry with 'em sight-seein', but they were
> some acquainted with foreign lands an' their laws. . . . They got some

29. This term is from Abdul R. JanMohamed, who defines it as a tendency of
a writer to get locked into an ideology that limits a particular group to a romantic
past that permanently anachronizes it. I argue that affirmation overshadows this
tendency even though characters like Captain Littlepage are clearly locked in the
past. See JanMohamed, *Manichean Aesthetics: The Politics of Literature in Colonial
Africa* (Amherst, 1983). Critics who see Jewett as nostalgically stuck in the past
include Wood, "Literature of Impoverishment"; Berthoff, "Jewett's *Pointed Firs*";
and Pry, "Folk-Literary Aesthetics."

> sense o' proportion. . . . Shipping's a terrible loss to this part of New
> England from a social point o' view. (25)

It is somewhat problematic that these observations come from the most eccentric character in the text. The narrator is aware of his mental wanderings, yet she is also familiar with "the decadence of shipping interests" (32). Thus she agrees with Mrs. Todd, who acknowledges that some of his "tales hangs together toler'ble well" (33). That she chooses Mrs. Todd rather than the captain as her guide, however, suggests that this account is a "little page" in proportion to the entire story of the region. Though there is some justification for his feelings that "the worst have got to be best and rule everything" and that "we're all turned upside down and going back year by year," the herbalist's vision of strength and survival is more compelling. He laments that "there's no large-minded way of thinking now" (26), but the text of *Pointed Firs* negates his point through the affirmative, encompassing perspective of characters such as Mrs. Todd. Indeed, Jewett's own vision calls for a sense of proportion that should validate the reality of the male perspective but would also affirm the value of the often marginalized and devalued feminine perspective.

In the narrative of Joanna Todd, we confront another story of personal loss. Whereas Captain Littlepage articulates the story of economic loss that has fallen upon the region, Joanna articulates the spiritual loss of one who has abandoned the community to live in solitude. As the village recluse, she is another sign of the loss of balance and perspective. And once again, Jewett places a character in a physical setting that both mirrors her personality and comments on her adjustment to the past. Thus it is appropriate that she lives on Shell-heap Island, a barren, desolate area that is almost inaccessible to outsiders and is described as a "dreadful small place to make a world of." Her choice of this place reflects the inner barrenness she felt when her fiancé abandoned her. According to Mrs. Fosdick, Joanna had "all her hopes . . . built on marryin', an' having' a real home and somebody to look up to."

When the marriage did not come to fruition, she "acted just like a bird when its nest is spoilt" (61–62). In response to those who try to get her to leave Shell-heap Island, she says: "I haven't got no right to live with folks no more. . . . You must never ask me again. . . . I've done the only thing I could do and I've made my choice. I feel great comfort in your [Mrs. Todd's] kindness, but I don't deserve it. I have committed the unpardonable sin. . . . I was in great wrath and trouble, and my thoughts was so wicked towards God that I can't expect ever to be forgiven. I have come to know what it is to have patience, but I have lost hope. . . . I want to be alone" (70).

These are the words of one who has lost a sense of proportion, perspective, and balance. Joanna exhibits an image of spiritual loss that comes not only from a loss of hope but from a sense of personal failure. As one critic explains, "Besieged by the overpowering demands of marriage and theology, Joanna cannot forgive herself for having failed either one."[30] Like Captain Littlepage, she becomes trapped in her own limited imagination. Her self-imposed exile is both a retreat into solitude and a desperate bid for freedom from societal obligations.[31] Even though some, like Mrs. Fosdick, consider her a "great fool" who could think of no other way to "mend her troubles except to run off and hide" (65), she is nevertheless heroic. She confronts the reality of romantic rejection with the coping response of a woman who shapes experience on her own terms with the dignity and integrity of "one of the saints of the desert" (73).

Though Joanna chooses her hermitage as a response to loss, there is the slightest hint of something positive coming from her solitary experience, for her solitude gives her the freedom to "live alone with poor insistent human nature and the calms and passions of the sea and sky" (75). In addition, she gives full rein to ingenuity by gathering rushes from a nearby swamp to braid

---

30. Johns, "'Mateless and Appealing.'"
31. Pearson and Pope, *Female Hero in American and British Literature,* 47.

beautiful mats for her floor and a cushion for her bunk. Her crafts
not only show a "good deal of invention" (68), but they suggest
the value of solitude. As the narrator observes, "Later generations
will know less and less of Joanna herself, but there are paths
trodden to shrines of solitude the world over,—the world cannot
forget them" (75).

In paying homage to Joanna in particular and to solitude in
general, the narrator affirms her own connection to this recluse
while elevating her to mythic status. Moreover, when we recall
the narrator's own desire for solitude in returning to Dunnet
Landing, it is clear that she identifies with Joanna's desire for it.
When she first arrives, she complains that the "one fault . . . with
this choice of a summer lodging place . . . was its complete lack
of seclusion" (13–14). Because her early intention was to seek the
refuge of this rural village so she could write, it is clear that she
understands how freedom from society can empower one to create. We are reminded of Jewett's advice to Willa Cather that the
writer is the "only artist who must be a solitary . . . who need[s]
to have time to [her]self . . . to read and add to [her] recognitions."[32] Thus in the portrait of Joanna, Jewett not only inscribes
the tragedy of a uniquely personal yet feminine loss, but she also
inscribes a mythic identification between the recluse and all those
who would defy society for the sake of personal freedom and to
empower the self.

No discussion of *Pointed Firs* is complete that does not acknowledge that the narrator not only provides a unifying perspective and aesthetic complexity to the text but also serves as a kind
of surrogate reader of this regional landscape that Jewett seeks to
inscribe in fiction. As the narrator/protagonist, she both observes
and participates in the plot. Indeed, the entire narrative is essentially the story of her initiation into the world of Dunnet Landing.
Though she sees her visit as a flight from an urban prison of complexity and a return to a rural haven of simplicity, her initiation

32. Fields, ed., *Letters of Jewett*, 250.

challenges her preconceived notions about simplicity and raises her consciousness to accept dimensions of country life she never suspected. Once she begins meeting the people, learning their individual and collective histories, and participating in their rituals, she realizes there is more to the village than picturesque scenery. In her role as protagonist, she moves through three phases of development in perspective: from detachment characterized by ignorance and superiority, to involvement characterized by experience and acceptance, and finally to enlightenment characterized by knowledge and understanding. In her role as narrator, she is the device Jewett employs to provide her readers with a corresponding transformed insight into country life. Rather than focus on surface peculiarities, she draws on the cultural roots of this landscape. Hence the emphasis on people, their expressions, habits, stories, and rituals. Structurally, the novel begins with a funeral, climaxes with a family reunion, and ends with a wedding. Beneath this structure there occurs a gradual process of transformation.

In the early days of her visit, the narrator constantly reminds herself and the villagers that she does "not really belong to Dunnet Landing" (21). She faithfully escapes the people's "quaint" oddities and retreats to the schoolhouse to write, aware of her position as both "small scholar" and "great authority," yet valuing the advantages of her "retired situation" (18). She gradually drops her defenses, however, and becomes less of an observer and more of a participant. This movement corresponds to the climax of the novel—the Bowden family reunion.

It is at the Bowden reunion that the narrator seems most involved with the people. In addition to the intimacy she develops with Mrs. Todd, there is also her close relationship with Mrs. Blackett (Mrs. Todd's mother), her brother William, and other friends and family members. The intimacy she begins to experience prompts her to feel less like a visitor and more "like an adopted Bowden" (89). The affinity she begins to feel with these people is represented in her shift from first-person singular pronoun references—"I"—to first-person plural "we":

> We might have been a company of ancient Greeks going to celebrate a victory, or to worship a god of harvest in the grove above. It was strangely moving to see this and to make part of it. The sky, the sea, have watched poor humanity at its rites so long; we were no more than a New England family celebrating its own existence and simple progress; we carried the tokens and inheritance of all such households from which this had descended, and were only the latest of our line. We possessed the instincts of a far, forgotten childhood; I found myself thinking that we ought to be carrying green branches and singing as we went. (90)

This passage suggests another change that the narrator undergoes. She chooses not to regard these villagers as mere rustic folk or to trivialize their ways. Instead, she comes to respect them for maintaining integrity in spite of the harsh realities of their lives—realities she once had not seen or had ignored. Moreover, in speaking of the Greek chorus, she alludes both to the grandeur and the tragedy of these people she has grown to understand. Her reflections on Mrs. Todd are particularly poignant and indicative of the respect with which she now regards these people: "I could see that sometimes when Mrs. Todd had seemed limited and heavily domestic, she had simply grown sluggish for lack of proper surroundings. . . . It was not the first time I was full of wonder at the waste of human ability in this world. . . . More than one face among the Bowdens showed that only opportunity and stimulus were lacking,—a narrow set of circumstances had caged a fine able character and held it captive" (95). Perhaps nowhere is the ironic nature of Jewett's portrayal of characters and setting more apparent. Even those who heroically eke out a living are clearly held captive in this rural landscape.

This revelation leads to the final phase of the narrator's transformation—that of enlightenment. The final chapter is appropriately titled "A Backward View," for despite her initiation, the narrator realizes that she cannot remain in this landscape. Though she fears she will be a "foreigner" (158) when she returns to the city, she nevertheless must leave the region she has come to value.

As in other Jewett stories of flight and return, the memory of her excursion is a token of her experiences. Unlike Mrs. Todd, the narrator is not held captive to a narrow set of circumstances but is free both literally and through the art of her writing to come and go as she pleases. Her experience parallels that of Jewett in that she uses the creative process to inscribe and describe the cultural roots of a people and place in an aesthetic search for truth. As Ann Douglas Wood observes: "This search [of an author and narrator for material], and the resulting self-consciousness, are major, although subtle themes in the book. We watch her quite literally interviewing candidates for characterization, we hear her test out descriptions, we see her secluding herself to write. She cannot stay in Dunnet Landing, but she can write about it. She cannot become Mrs. Todd, but she can possess her by using her life as the vital center of her story."[33] In constructing a narrative fence around Dunnet Landing, the narrator not only gains possession of Mrs. Todd, a region, and a way of life, but she responds to the forgotten time they represent with a greater sense of perspective and recognition of complexity. Nevertheless, we cannot escape the narrator's problematic position. Despite the intersubjective moments when she both recognizes and identifies with Mrs. Todd and others as subjects in their own right, the very process of writing about them raises the possibility that she will reify them as objects, as "others" who are subject to her gaze as privileged outsider. To render them and their stories in writing, therefore, is to risk the very commodification that denies their subjectivity.[34]

Yet the title of the final chapter signifies the clarity of vision that can accompany a retrospective look at time and experience. As the summer ends and the narrator takes a final look at the landscape, she realizes that "the sea, the sky, all along the shore

33. Wood, "Literature of Impoverishment," 29.
34. For two excellent analyses of the problematic relationship between self and other, see Benjamin, *Bonds of Love*, 221–24, and Helena Michie, "Not One of the Family: The Repression of the Other Woman in Feminist Theory," in *Discontented Discourses: Feminism, Textual Intervention, and Psychoanaysis,* ed. Marleen S. Barr and Richard Feldstein (Urbana, 1989), 15–28.

line and the inland hills, with every bush of bay and every fir-top, gained a deeper color and a sharper clearness" (157). Her observation of the setting mirrors her deeper appreciation and sharper perspective toward the people of the region as well. Yet a stark counterpoint to this thought seems to rupture the transformed vision, for the very next paragraph contains a regret: "I wished to have one of my first weeks back again, with those long hours when nothing happened except the growth of herbs and the course of the sun. Once I had not even known where to go for a walk; now there are many delightful things to be done and done again" (157–58). The narrator is attempting to regain her former innocence, but in the reference to herbs, which recalls Mrs. Todd, and in the reference to walks and things to do, which recalls the rituals she has enjoyed, it becomes clear that her perspective has been revised, her consciousness permanently transformed. Though the village appears to sink "back into the uniformity of the coast and [become] indistinguishable from the other towns" (160), the narrator has committed the reality of its uniqueness to memory. Yet the story she tells affirms both the commonness and the magic of the landscape. What becomes lost to sight cannot be lost to memory or desire.

Thus, through the narrator, Jewett constructs a fictive fence around a time and place she wants her reader to remember and respect. By drawing on and connecting the folk and mythic roots of her native region, she seeks to revise cultural attitudes and transform the consciousness of those who would devalue their significance or marginalize their literary potential. Ultimately, she affirms their secure place in the texture of American experience. The complexity of her affirmative response in *The Country of the Pointed Firs* stems from the numerous contradictions inherent in her recognitions. As one critic asserts, however, American literature "springs from contradictions."[35] The achievement of Sarah Orne Jewett's fiction is that she did not seek to deny those contradictions but instead to hold them in balance.

35. Berthoff, "Jewett's *Pointed Firs*," 50.

3

MYTH AS USABLE PAST: AFFIRMATION OF COMMUNITY AND SELF IN *SONG OF SOLOMON*

> To read is to find meanings and to find meanings is to name them; but these named meanings are swept away toward further names; names invoke each other . . . I name, I unname, I rename.
> —Roland Barthes, *S/Z*

> The act of writing requires a constant plunging back into the shadow of the past where time hovers ghostlike.
> —Ralph Ellison, *Shadow and Act*

> Pilate can't teach you a thing you can use in this world. Maybe the next, but not this one.
> —Toni Morrison, *Song of Solomon*

At the heart of Toni Morrison's *Song of Solomon* (1977) is a nexus of myth and folklore that is deeply rooted in African-American history and culture. In fact, it is difficult to discuss her fiction without alluding to myth, folklore, or both. Unfortunately, much of the criticism of *Song of Solomon* has tended to focus more on myth in a strict literary sense and less on folklore or the profound cultural context on which her writing is based.[1] This discussion attempts to bring a more comprehensive reading to that text— one that recognizes Morrison's expressed narrative intentions of affirming the complexity of African-American experience and

1. Some of the studies that have discussed *Song of Solomon* from a mythic perspective include de Weever, "Toni Morrison's Use of Fairy Tale"; Harris, "Myth as Structure," 69–76; Wilfred D. Samuels, "Liminality and the Search for Self in Toni Morrison's *Song of Solomon*," *Minority Voices*, V (1981), 59–68; and Gerry Brenner, "*Song of Solomon*: Rejecting Rank's Monomyth and Feminism," in *Critical Essays on Toni Morrison*, ed. Nellie McKay (Boston, 1988), 114–25.

analyzes the complex and powerful ways in which *Song of Solomon* bears witness to these intentions.

Some of the best clues to Morrison's narrative intentions can be found in interviews she has given over the past ten years. First and foremost is her concern with language and the unique ways in which her people use it. In her words, she wants "to restore the language that Black people spoke to its original power."[2] For her that means turning to the folktales, gossip, music, myth, and other manifestations of the oral tradition. She reminisces that "the myths are misunderstood now because we [black people] are not talking to each other the way I was spoken to when I was growing up in a very small town. You knew everything in that little microcosm. But we don't live where we were born. . . . So the myths get forgotten."[3]

This oral tradition also contains a cosmology that she seeks to embed in her fiction:

> I could blend the acceptance of the supernatural and profound root-edness in the real world at the same time with neither taking precedence over the other. It is indicative of the cosmology, the way in which Black people looked at the world. We are very practical people, very down-to-earth, even shrewd people. But within that practicality we also accepted what I suppose could be called superstition and magic which is another way of knowing things. But to blend those two worlds together at the same time was enhancing, not limiting. And

2. Le Clair, "Language Must Not Sweat," 26. Other useful interviews include Morrison, "Rootedness," 339–45; Charles Ruas, *Conversations with American Writers* (New York, 1985), 215–43; Gloria Naylor and Toni Morrison, "A Conversation," *Southern Review*, XXI (1985), 567–93; Audrey McCluskey, "A Conversation with Toni Morrison," in *Women in the Arts: A Celebration* (Bloomington, 1986), 82–88; Nellie McKay, "An Interview with Toni Morrison, *Contemporary Literature*, XXIV (1983), 416–17; Claudia Tate, "Toni Morrison," in *Black Women Writers at Work*, ed. Tate (New York, 1983), 117–31; Robert Stepto, "'Intimate Things in Place': A Conversation with Toni Morrison," in *Chant of Saints*, ed. Michael S. Harper and Robert B. Stepto (Chicago, 1979), 213–29.

3. Le Clair, "Language Must Not Sweat," 26.

some of those things were "discredited knowledge" that Black people had; discredited only because Black people were discredited [and] therefore what they *knew* was "discredited."[4]

Inherent in this blend of myth and fact, or the magic with the real, is Morrison's own knowledge and understanding of past and present African-American experience. She brings a sense of history to her fiction that, combined with myth and folklore, reveals the "accumulated collective reality" that Alice Walker feels is lacking in much black literature.[5]

For this reason, contrary to most critical discussions, which focus on Milkman Dead, the protagonist of *Song of Solomon,* and his quest for identity, I believe a dual analysis is more consistent with Morrison's own narrative intentions and aesthetic.[6] Morrison sees myth in a broad sense, as usable past that she can consciously draw on to affirm the existential quest of the self as well as to affirm those folk processes that give coherence to black people as a collective entity or community. The source of this coherence lies in the ways these folk processes both challenge and subvert the established order of middle-class values which seek to discredit and suppress them.[7] Through her portrayal of Milkman Dead and the community into which he is born and from which he flees,

---

4. Morrison, "Rootedness," 342.

5. Walker, "From an Interview," in Walker, *In Search of Our Mothers' Gardens,* 262. One of the best discussions of Morrison's use of history is in Willis, "Eruptions of Funk." Also see Susan Willis, *Specifying: Black Women Writing the American Experience* (Madison, 1987).

6. Most discussions that focus on myth analyze *Song of Solomon* in terms of Milkman's quest for identity. I see Morrison using this quest as a tool in *two* directions—toward the individual and the community. Other noteworthy studies that focus on the quest pattern are Valerie Smith, "The Quest for and Discovery of Identity in Toni Morrison's *Song of Solomon," Southern Review,* XXI (1975), 721–32; and Peter Bruck, "Returning to One's Roots: The Motif of Searching and Flying in Toni Morrison's *Song of Solomon,"* in *The Afro-American Novel Since 1960,* ed. Peter Bruck and Wolfgang Karrer (Amsterdam, 1982), 289–305.

7. Alan Dundes, *Interpreting Folklore* (Bloomington, 1980), 8.

Morrison echoes James Baldwin's truism that "the past is all that makes the present coherent."[8]

Although scholars do not agree on a precise definition of myth and folklore is often subsumed under it as though *myth* were a generic term, I suggest two working definitions.[9] Myth can be defined simply as the collection of stories that appeal to the deep consciousness of a people or culture by embodying their rites and themes through the supernatural yet tragic and comic feats of heroic figures. Folklore differs from myth in that it is the vernacular expression of beliefs, customs, and traditions that identify a particular people. Because Morrison structures her novel around mythic patterns of questing and searching that recall not only the African-American past but classical mythology, *Song of Solomon* exemplifies her mythic impulse. Hence the elements of ritual associated with the heroic quest are part of Milkman's story. At the same time, however, Morrison narrates his story through the language of African and African-American folklore. Hence the oral tradition, vernacular expressions, naming customs, and folk music are all part of Milkman's story as well. But neither myth nor folklore is static. Myth is both usable form and a process by which Morrison could affirm what the larger culture had discredited or marginalized by appropriating, revising, and reshaping that form for her fiction. Likewise, folklore is not a collection of things or commodities but a communication process that operates within a given cultural context. My approach to Morrison follows the analytical method that Robert Hemenway proposes be used more often to discuss African-American literature, that is, the method of folk-literary analysis in which the scholar isolates the folkloric representation in the literary text; identifies by corroborating its authenticity; studies the communication context to the extent that information is available; examines the literary context to deter-

---

8. James Baldwin, *Notes of a Native Son* (New York, 1955), 4.

9. See Lévi-Strauss, *The Raw and the Cooked*, 3; Chase, *Quest for Myth*, 97; Campbell, *Hero with a Thousand Faces*, 382; Frazer, *Golden Bough*, 824–26; and Bettleheim, *Uses of Enchantment*, 35–40.

mine what vestiges of oral communication seem to have been used; considers the ways in which the author transformed and adapted the folkloric phenomena (including text, texture, and context); and interprets the literary text in light of all the information obtained.[10]

For Morrison, historical changes such as black migration to urban areas, assimilation into the middle class, and acculturation to Western values have threatened the old values that once gave cultural coherence to black people's lives. She feels that her novels can address these changes:

> I think long and carefully about what my novels ought to do. They should clarify the roles that have become obscured; they ought to identify those things in the past that are useful and those things that are not; and they ought to give nourishment. . . . The novel . . . tells about the city values, the urban values. Now my people, we "peasants," have come to the city, that is to say, we live with its values. There is a confrontation between old values of the tribes and new urban values. It's confusing . . . I am not explaining anything to anybody. My work bears witness and suggests who the outlaws were, who survived under what circumstances and why, what was legal in the community as opposed to what was legal outside it.[11]

Morrison's fiction, therefore, is a response to the loss of tradition, ways of knowing, and ways of perceiving oneself and the world. *Song of Solomon* bears witness to these lost and discredited traditions by incorporating "mythology . . . [to] provide what the culture did."[12] It is when Milkman discovers, understands, and respects these traditions that he discovers the meaning of his name, his own life, and his familial past.

10. Dan Ben-Amos, "Toward a Definition of Folklore in Context," *Journal of American Folklore,* LXXXIV (1971), 9; Robert Hemenway, "Are You a Flying Lark or a Setting Dove?" in *Afro-American Literature,* ed. Fisher and Stepto, 122–52.

11. Le Clair, "Language Must Not Sweat," 26.

12. Ruas, *Conversations with American Writers,* 238.

The original title of *Song of Solomon* was *Milkman Dead*.[13] Although Morrison does not explain why she changed the title, it may be related to the interconnections among myth, folklore, history, and culture. In an interview before the publication of the novel, her statements about the success of another black woman writer, Gayl Jones, suggest the direction she wants her own writing to take: "There's that incredible kind of movement which yields an artistic representation of something that one takes for granted in history. I think that accounts for the success of Gayl Jones' first book, where you have the weight of history working itself out in the life of one, two, three people; I mean a large idea, brought down small, and at home, which gives it a universality and a particularity which makes it extraordinary."[14]

Although feminist scholars have made us aware that the concept of universality often perpetuates false notions of objectivity familiar to male hegemonic thought, Morrison links it with particularity to signify the value of historicizing representations of black life and culture. The achievement of *Song of Solomon* is that at the same time that it treats the individual quest of one man, Milkman Dead, it also devotes full attention to the larger historical and cultural context that makes such a quest possible. Consequently, like Sarah Orne Jewett, Morrison transforms the meaning of universality to challenge the values and assumptions her readers might take for granted.[15]

Indeed, it is Morrison's attempt to balance the universal and the

13. Stepto, "Intimate Things in Place," in *Chant of Saints,* ed. Harper and Stepto, 229. When Stepto interviewed Morrison in New York City on May 19, 1976, she said that the title of her new novel would be *Milkman Dead. Song of Solomon* was published nearly a year and a half later.

14. *Ibid.*

15. Poet Adrienne Rich argues that women are "not trying to become part of the old order misnamed 'universal' which has tabooed us; we are transforming the meaning of 'universality.'" See Elly Bulkin, "An Interview with Adrienne Rich: Part II," *Conditions: Two,* October, 1977, p. 58. For other critiques of universality, see *Making a Difference: Feminist Literature Criticism,* ed. Gayle Greene and Coppelia Kahn (London, 1985).

particular that makes *Song of Solomon* such a challenge for the reader. We have only to note how many critical discussions of the novel describe it as complex. On one hand, Morrison's meandering narrative strategy imitates the oral tradition in the language and style of a folktale. On the other, the plethora of names, the shifting chronology, the excessive dialogue, and the layers of individual and personal histories create a mosaic of narrative that makes meaning seem elusive. In fact, the reader's task is not unlike that of Milkman Dead, who must find the meaning in his complicated life story.[16] For the sake of clarity, a brief plot summary can help establish the essential elements of the narrative.

★ *Song of Solomon* is essentially the story of Milkman Dead's search for and discovery of meaning in his life. The two parts of the novel correspond to the fundamental realities with which he must come to terms: his community and his family history. Part I treats his current relationships with others and thus represents the present. Part II, which treats Milkman's confrontation with the incoherent and fragmented stories that others share with him about his ancestry, represents the past. In Part I we learn that he was born the day after the black community's insurance man, Mr. Smith, committed suicide in an apparent attempt to fly from the roof of the hospital. The song that is sung at the time of his "flight" is actually the song of the myth of the flying African, the puzzling song that Milkman will later have to decipher if he is to understand the story of his ancestors. We then learn of the loveless marriage of his parents, Macon Dead II and Ruth, of the contrived circumstances that led to his conception, of his mother's unnatural act of nursing him well into his fourth year, of the neighborhood gossip's discovery of this act as the origin of his losing his birth name, Macon Dead III, and being given the nickname "Milkman" (15), and of his father's position as the most "propertied

16. Linda W. Wagner uses the word *mosaic* to describe the narrative design of Toni Morrison's first novel, *The Bluest Eye*. See Wagner, "Toni Morrison: Mastery of Narrative," in *Contemporary American Women Writers,* ed. Catherine Rainwater and William J. Scheick (Lexington, 1985), 191–207.

Negro" (20) in town. We also learn of his eccentric aunt Pilate, of her daughter Reba, and of Reba's daughter Hagar, all of whom Macon calls a "collection of lunatics" (20) because they embarrass him.

Also in Part I we learn of Milkman's alienation from his two sisters, Magdalene, called Lena, and First Corinthians, of his alienation from almost everyone but his close friend Guitar Bains, the leader of a quasi-political gang, and of his prolonged but disinterested love affair with Hagar, his cousin. In addition, we learn of his parents' respective guilt-ridden attempts to explain the past to him, of his decision to end his affair with Hagar, and of her subsequent monthly attempts to kill him. Most important, at the end of Part I we learn of his attempt, with assistance from Guitar, to steal a bag from Pilate which his father leads him to believe contains his inheritance of gold, of his discovery that this bag contains only human bones and not gold, and of his subsequent decision to leave home and head south in part to search for the gold but primarily to flee from the urban milieu and the responsibilities and entanglements of family, friendship, and love so that he could "live [his] own life" (222). This decision, which comes at the end of the nine rather lengthy chapters of Part I, becomes the impetus for Milkman's journey to the rural home of his ancestors, a journey which is narrated in the six short chapters of Part II.

Milkman's journey in Part II takes him first to a small Pennsylvania town where he inquires about Circe, the midwife who cared for his father and aunt when their mother, Sing, died in childbirth. His inquiry leads him to a group of men who share their memories of Macon Dead in a series of storytelling rituals. He then finds Circe, the dreamy, witchlike figure who helps him discover more pieces of his familial past, who helps him make sense of the fragmented versions he got from Macon and Pilate, and who tells him the location of the cave where his grandfather's body had been dumped. Unsuccessful at finding either the body or the gold in the cave, Milkman decides the gold must be in Virginia, the state from which his grandparents had migrated to the North.

Once he arrives in Shalimar, Virginia, his search takes on all the characteristics of an initiation rite into manhood. He participates in a verbal battle known as the "dozens," he defends himself in a physical knife and bottle challenge, he becomes a member of a hunting expedition, he experiences genuine sensuality for the first time, he deciphers the hidden meaning of his ancestral song, he endures the betrayal of friendship, and he discovers that his true inheritance is not gold but a legacy of his great-grandfather's heroic flight from oppression back to Africa. In the process of discovering that there is no gold to be found, he learns that the bones Pilate claims are her inheritance are actually the bones of her father, who was killed by whites when he tried to save his farm. Finally, Part II ends with his return to Michigan just long enough to get Pilate, whom he takes back to Virginia to give her father's remains a proper burial, with his recitation of his ancestral song to Pilate just before she dies, and with his ambiguous yet symbolic gesture of reunion with his friend Guitar at the end of the novel.

What this synopsis of *Song of Solomon* does not reveal is the prodigious sense of history and culture that informs the novel. Nor does it do justice to the complex intricacies of language and narrative with which Morrison writes. It is easier to appreciate the achievement of this novel if the analysis is divided into the two perspectives suggested by its two-part structure. Part I illustrates the folk aesthetic in that it focuses on the black community into which Milkman is born and on the means by which that community gives itself coherence. Part II illustrates the mythic impulse in that it focuses on Milkman's individual quest for identity and meaning. Although the first part seems disproportionately long, the disproportion correlates with Morrison's overriding interest in using narrative to affirm a discredited people and marginalized culture.[17] Together Parts I and II illustrate how the consciousness of the individual self can be transformed through the narrative act of storytelling. According to her folk aesthetic and mythic impulse, narrative can be used to suggest how such a cul-

17. *Ibid.*, 200.

ture could be transformed from within and without by reclaiming its forgotten myths, traditions, and values.

In the opening scene of *Song of Solomon,* Robert Smith, an insurance agent, adorns himself with wings, goes to the roof of Mercy Hospital, and leaps to his death the day before Macon "Milkman" Dead III is born in 1931. Although Milkman does not connect this event with his own life until much later, Morrison uses this scene to establish the character of the black community into which this bizarre death and significant birth occur and to introduce the white community by implication rather than explicit portrayal. From the outset, Morrison also establishes the network of history and culture within which Mr. Smith's suicide occurs. She evokes American aviation history by comparing the small crowd that witnesses Mr. Smith's flight to the larger crowd drawn by "Lindbergh . . . four years earlier" (3). Implicit in the comparison are the larger historical differences between the circumstances that motivate the two men's respective desires to fly. This signification through naming will be discussed in more detail, but the point here is that it is both a rhetorical device and a theme of the novel. Morrison's insertion of Lindbergh's name is a means of evoking history while serving as a critique of history in which flight occurs for disparate reasons. Mr. Smith's flight is a sign of escape from racial injustice; Lindbergh's is a heroic expression of creativity, ingenuity, and freedom. As we learn later in the novel, Mr. Smith's suicide is a response to his inability to cope with the hatred and secrecy required for membership in the Seven Days, a gang formed to avenge the murder of black people through random killing of white people. Yet by the end of the novel, as Morrison eloquently argues in a recent essay, we can read Mr. Smith's "flight" in heroic terms as well, as a commitment made, a promise kept, and a sign of his connection to African and African-American myths about "black people who could fly."[18]

18. See Toni Morrison, "Unspeakable Things Unspoken: The Afro-American Presence in American Literature," *Michigan Quarterly Review,* XXVIII (1989), 1–34; and Le Clair, "Language Must Not Sweat," 27. Morrison acknowledges

American history is also evoked in references to racial exclusionary practices in housing, when "the only colored doctor in the city" (4) became the first to live on Mains Avenue in 1896, in references to the military, when 1918 is the year "colored men were being drafted" (4), and in allusions to medical services, when, in 1931, Milkman was the "first colored" (4) child born at Mercy Hospital. In chapter 3, Morrison evokes history more directly through a barbershop scene in which a group of men are listening to a radio newscast about an apparently racially motivated murder. In the words of the text: "A young Negro boy had been stomped to death in Sunflower County, Mississippi. . . . His name was Till" (80). Clearly, this is an allusion to the early 1950s murder of a fourteen-year-old black youth named Emmett Till.[19] This murder has historical significance because it "became a worldwide symbol of Southern racism, a spark that helped ignite the civil rights movement."[20] Yet we are not to construe such facts and pieces of history as attempts to validate the entire novel. Morrison's comments about her brief foray into playwriting are instructive: "I like to make up stuff. . . . I take scraps, the landscape of something that happened, and make up the rest. I'm not interested in documentaries. I'm not sticking to the facts.[21] Although these remarks refer to Morrison's play *Dreaming Emmett,* they could easily be applied to *Song of Solomon.* In the novel, we

---

that the myth of the flying African might seem silly, but she says it is part of the folklore of her life to accept flying as one of the gifts her people, meaning black people, had.

19. Apparently Morrison's interest in the Emmett Till murder runs very deep, for in 1985 she wrote a play based on the same case. The play, called *Dreaming Emmett,* is one she conceived to show "a collision of three or four levels of time through the eyes of one person who could come back to life and seek vengeance." For a review of this play and Morrison's writing of it, see Margaret Croyden, "Toni Morrison Tries Her Hand at Playwriting," New York *Times,* December 29, 1985, Sec. H, p. 6. For a more specific reference to this case, see *Song of Solomon,* 111.

20. Croyden, "Toni Morrison Tries Her Hand at Playwriting," 6.

21. *Ibid.,* 16.

are to read her allusions to fact in two ways: as signs of the historical resources upon which her fiction is based and as signs of the intersection between individual and collective history.

Even more significant than the historical resources that inform *Song of Solomon,* however, are the cultural resources that Morrison consciously draws upon to give authenticity to her depiction of the black community. These cultural resources form the basis of her folk aesthetic, and through them she records the inner workings of the community as well as its imaginative responses to the vagaries of history. The first sign of the folk aesthetic appears early in the novel in the phrase "word-of-mouth news" (3), which describes how some members of the community learn about Mr. Smith's promise to fly from the roof of Mercy Hospital. But the phrase also signifies the function Morrison wants language to serve in her novels: "There are things I try to incorporate into my fiction that are directly and deliberately related to what I regard as the major characteristics of Black art . . . one of which is the ability to be both print and oral literature: to combine those two aspects so that the stories can be read in silence, of course, but one should be able to hear them as well."[22] She views her fiction as a written replacement of the "word-of-mouth news" or oral tradition she feels has been lost, or at least devalued in the wake of historical changes. Therefore, the phrase *word-of-mouth* is both form and substance in that it is a sign of the folk aesthetic she wants to affirm at the same time that it is the very substance that gives meaning and shape to her novel.

The second important sign of the folk aesthetic in *Song of Solomon* is that of names and naming. Indeed, it is the complicated nexus of names that forms the crux of the identity theme that runs throughout the novel. As Morrison explains: "The name thing is a very, very strong theme in the book . . . the absence of a name given at all, the odd names and the slave names, the whole business, the feeling of anonymity, the feeling of orphanage."[23]

22. Morrison, "Rootedness," 341.

23. Stepto, "Intimate Things in Place," in *Chant of Saints,* ed. Harper and Stepto, 226.

Morrison's theme of names and naming establishes an intertextual relationship between her novel and Ralph Ellison's *Invisible Man* in which anonymity and the absence of a name shape the hero's quest and inform the design of the narrative.[24] Although there are sharp differences between the two texts and between the journeys of the two protagonists, Morrison's use of names bears witness to Ellison's pronouncement on their significance in "Hidden Name and Complex Fate": "We must learn to wear our names within all the noise and confusion of the environment in which we find ourselves; make them the center of all our associations with the world, with man and with nature. We must charge them with all our emotions, our hopes, hates, loves, aspirations. They must become our masks and our shields and the containers of all those values and traditions which we learn and/or imagine as being the meaning of our familial past."[25] A closer look at how naming operates in *Song of Solomon* reveals that names not only form a historical and cultural index to the past but also empower the community and the individual to shape and affirm their own experiences.

Naming is first introduced into the text in the rather elaborate explanation of how "Not Doctor Street" (4) got its name. Although the street is registered in the town as Mains Avenue, patients of the city's first "colored" doctor began calling it "Doctor

24. The intertextual relationship between Ellison and Morrison deserves a great deal more attention than I can give it here. In many ways, *Song of Solomon* is a response to and revision of *Invisible Man*. Morrison revises the existential journey from invisibility to the alienated self with a journey from the alienated self to the affirmation of self and community. Acts of naming and being supersede running and escaping, though both novels contain these elements. The journey from North to South replaces the escape from South to North. For an excellent analysis of intertextual revision in the African-American literary tradition, see Henry Louis Gates, Jr., "The Blackness of Blackness: A Critique of the Sign and the Signifying Monkey," in *Black Literature,* ed. Gates, 151–72. For a more recent analysis of the intertextual relationship between Morrison's novels and Ellison's, see Michael Awkward, *Inspiriting Influences: Tradition, Revision, and Afro-American Women's Novels* (New York, 1989).

25. Ellison, *Shadow and Act,* 151.

Street" when he moved there. Thus the name is a recognition of history and an affirmation of that segment of the community that gives it validity through continued use. But when the post office refuses to recognize the name and places all mail addressed to Doctor Street in the "Dead Letter Office," the power of the name begins to fade. For a short time it is revived with quasi-official status when "colored" recruits register for the draft and give Doctor Street as their address. But eventually the city legislators see to it that the name is "never used in any official capacity" (4) by posting public notices that proclaim that the street "would always be known as Mains Avenue and not Doctor Street" (4).

The response of the community to this public notice is particularly interesting, for it places the entire sequence of events in perspective at the same time that it suggests Morrison's narrative intent: "It was a genuinely clarifying notice because it gave Southside residents a way to keep their memories alive and please the city legislators as well. They called it Not Doctor Street, and were inclined to call the charity hospital at its northern end No Mercy Hospital since it was 1931, on the day following Mr. Smith's leap from its cupola before the first colored expectant mother was allowed to give birth inside its wards and not on its steps" (4–5). Inherent in the process of Mains Avenue becoming Not Doctor Street and Mercy Hospital becoming No Mercy Hospital is a critique of the established order as well as an expression of freedom from that order. As Keith Byerman argues: "Names have a concrete history; they keep alive the complex, painful, disorderly creative reality of human experience that dominant logocentric structures seek to oppress. They register the hidden expressions of life in defiance of the controlling word. They are also liberating and magical."[26] Hence the process of naming, unnaming, and renaming is an ironic assertion of authority, a recognition of the plurality of meaning, and a statement of self-affirmation.[27] In that

26. Keith Byerman, *Fingering the Jagged Grain: Tradition and Form in Recent Black Fiction* (Athens, Ga., 1985), 206.
27. Barthes, *S/Z*, 17–18.

the names of Macon Dead, Milkman, and Pilate all have concrete histories rooted in cultural traditions, they offer other examples of Morrison's folk aesthetic through naming. Moreover, these names are links in the narrative of the past that Milkman must decipher if he is to learn his identity.

Macon Dead is the head of the Dead family and as such his hateful coldness and fiery intimidation determine the loveless, sterile climate of the household. A proud man who harbors nothing but contempt for his wife, disappointment toward his daughters, disgust toward his sister, a selfish desire to control his son, and a lack of compassion for the tenants who reside in the housing units that have given him middle-class status, Macon Dead has a last name that aptly describes his emotional sensibility. Indeed, his character corresponds directly to the mythic god Hades, who presides over earthly riches and rides through the underworld in a chariot drawn by black horses.[28] Like his car, which the community both covets and envies by calling it "Macon Dead's hearse," Macon "had no real lived life at all" (33) outside of his ambitious pursuit of money and things expressed in his dictum to Milkman to "own things. And let the things you own own other things. Then you'll own yourself and other people too" (55). Unfortunately, Milkman unwittingly embraces the impoverished perspective and bourgeois values beneath this advice until he comes to terms with the real meaning of his life.

Yet despite this characterization of him as a spiritually dead man whose conspicuous consumption motivates him to exploit others at will, Macon has contemplative moments that partially redeem him. An example occurs early in the novel when he wonders whether "he and his sister had some ancestor . . . who had a name that was real . . . a name given . . . at birth with love and seriousness" (17). After hearing his son's distasteful nickname, he recalls the prophetic circumstances surrounding his own name, which he tries to explain to Milkman as "a literal slip of the pen

28. Graves, *Greek Myths,* I, 90.

handed to his father on a piece of paper" (18). This episode of misnaming occurred when a drunken Yankee soldier at the Freedmen's Bureau inadvertently wrote his birthplace and the whereabouts of his father in the spaces for his first and last names.[29] Because Macon's father "couldn't read, couldn't even sign his name" (53), the misname was recorded as his official name. Ironically, he did not attempt to correct the error because his wife convinced him that the new name "would wipe out the past" (54). Ellison refers to the attempt to signify the concept in general as an effort to "destroy the verbal evidence of a willed and ritualized discontinuity of blood and human intercourse" that overlooks the "triumph of spirit . . . of those who rallied, reassembled and transformed themselves and who under dismembering pressures refused to die."[30] Only after years of disregarding his father's account of this misnaming incident is Milkman able to piece together the details that lead him to his father's and grandfather's real name.

Milkman's nickname also has an extraordinary origin. Like the name Macon Dead, it is a misname imposed by someone with no concern about the consequences. Moreover, it is a name laden with family history, embarrassment, and shame, which Milkman never fully understands. His name is first a direct connection to his mother, Ruth. Morrison depicts Ruth as a "small woman" (124), whose life has been lived vicariously, first through her father, then through her husband. As the only child of Dr. Foster, the Negro doctor for whom Not Doctor Street was named, she is not so much a wife to Macon as an acquisition, a possession to enhance his privileged status in the community as "a colored man of property" (23). Like the goddess Persephone, whose abduction, rape, and subsequent marriage to Hades signify loss of status and feminine power, Ruth's marriage to Macon signifies a similar loss and submission to abusive power and male domination. In

29. Leslie H. Fishel and Benjamin Quarles, eds., *The Black American: A Documentary History* (Glenview, Ill., 1976), 259, 262, 269, 318–19.

30. Ellison, *Shadow and Act,* 152.

her sterile marriage the days are "stunned into stillness" (11) by his contempt. His failure to sleep with her after their daughters were born prompts her to consult his sister Pilate, herbal priestess and conjure woman, whose assistance results in Ruth's "single triumph" (133), the birth of Macon Dead III. The triumph of his birth is that he survived Macon's numerous attempts to make her abort. Though Macon's birth fails to rekindle the marriage, it represents Ruth's "one aggressive act brought to royal completion" (133).

The relationship between mother and son takes an unnatural turn in the form of a secret indulgence. Each day of his life well into his fourth year, Macon III satisfies his mother's indulgence by allowing her to nurse him at her breasts. The act is described as pushing her into "fantasy": "She had the distinct impression that his lips were pulling from her a thread of light. It was as though she were a cauldron issuing spinning gold. Like the miller's daughter—the one that sat at night in a straw-filled room, thrilled with the secret power Rumpelstiltskin had given her: to see golden thread stream from her very own shuttle. And that was the other part of her pleasure, a pleasure she hated to give up" (13–14). Clearly, Morrison's insertion of the Rumpelstiltskin fairy tale is no coincidence, for it reinforces the theme of naming and misnaming.[31] Ruth's pleasure goes awry and these afternoon rituals are confirmed as "strange and wrong" (14) when Freddie, the janitor and neighborhood gossip, discovers her in the act of nursing Milkman. Even though Macon refuses to acknowledge his son's nickname, it sticks because of the persistence of the community's continued word-of-mouth use. Morrison's elaborate telling of the mythic dimensions of Milkman's birth, name, and childhood gives the narrative a fairy-tale quality.

Pilate plays an integral role in Milkman's birth, a prophetic role that suggests her continued importance in his initiation into man-

---

31. *Grimms' Fairy Tales* (New York, 1985), 124–28. Also see de Weever, "Toni Morrison's Use of Fairy Tale."

hood. Thus it is appropriate that the origins of her name are just as unusual as those of Macon and Milkman. Pilate is described as one who literally wears her name; it was chosen in accordance with an old African-American tradition of selecting a newborn baby's name from the Bible.[32] Her father, who could not read or write, selected the name his finger pointed to first. Even though the midwife tried to advise him against the "Christ-killing Pilate" (19), he persisted, partially out of confusion and melancholy over his wife's death at childbirth. At the age of twelve, Pilate removed the paper that bears her name from the Bible, folded it up, and placed it in a tiny brass box which she wears as an earring. The fact that she wears her name suggests the value she places on her identity over her possessions—a quality that distinguishes her from her brother Macon. Her role as herbalist and conjure woman who saves Milkman's life is an ironic comment on her name, which is reiterated in the clue to the name of his ancestors contained in the song Milkman overhears her singing:

O Sugarman don't leave me here
Cotton balls to choke me
O Sugarman don't leave me here
Buckra's arms to yoke me . . .
Sugarman done fly away
Sugarman done gone
Sugarman cut across the sky
Sugarman gone home (49)

Neither Pilate's song nor the name repeated in it has any meaning for Milkman, however, until he separates himself from the community so he can understand it and his place within it.

But before he leaves the community he must prepare for his journey. Hence Part I is the narrative of Milkman's introduction into his family and community. The introduction is primarily ac-

32. Le Clair, "Language Must Not Sweat," 28.

complished through rituals of storytelling, and that is the third sign of Morrison's folk aesthetic in *Song of Solomon*.[33] As an essential element of the African-American oral tradition, storytelling is not only a vehicle for passing the history from one generation to the next but also the means by which the community gives itself coherence. The primary stories that give Milkman a sense of his community are those of Macon, Ruth, Guitar, and Pilate. Although the stories he hears from his sisters, Hagar, and the men in the neighborhood help to shape his consciousness to a certain extent, they are not nearly as important as the stories he hears from his parents, his best friend, and his aunt.

Macon essentially tells Milkman three stories—the story of his father, Macon Dead I, the story of his marriage to Ruth, and the story of the gold he believes Pilate has stolen from him. In the story of his own father, Macon shares his account of how his "father had . . . died protecting his property," a farm named Lincoln's Heaven (51). In this story he also mentions Circe, the midwife who cared for him and Pilate after their father's death, the circumstances surrounding the name, the fact that his mother "looked like a white woman," and the fact that both Pilate and his father "looked like all them pictures you ever see of Africans" (54). Macon shares this first story to convince Milkman that Pilate is "no good" (54), that she cannot teach him anything he "can use in this world" (55), and that he has a legacy of ownership in his family. Ironically, this story contains nothing that Milkman can use either, although it foreshadows the irony that Pilate *will* be able to teach him something—not in the urban world of acquisition, shallow living, and middle-class values but in the rural world of tradition and communal values.

The second story Macon shares is in reaction to Milkman's hitting him for striking Ruth. He prefaces his version of the story of their marriage by telling him he must "deal with the whole truth if he wants to be a whole man" (70). The "information" (70) that

33 Skerrett, "Recitation to the Griot," 199–202.

he goes on to share is of Ruth's father's disliking him, of his disgust because her father delivered their first two children, and of Ruth's unnatural and almost perverse display of affection toward her father's dead body. But Milkman does not want this information from his father. Rather than enlightening him, the story convinces him that "his whole family was a bunch of crazies" and that it is nothing more than "some way-out tale about how come and why" (76). This story raises more questions than it answers and prompts Milkman to question precisely why the story of his past is so confusing.

The third story Macon tells is his version about the gold found in the cave where his father's remains were reputed to be. In telling Milkman his story, he confesses that it is part of the first story that he "never finished," and that it explains why he calls Pilate "a snake" (165). According to this story, Pilate deceived Macon into leaving the cave so that she could get the tarpaulin containing gold. Macon shares this information with Milkman to entice him to go search for the gold. Rejecting the idea that Pilate's inheritance is anything but the gold, he promises Milkman that he can have half of it if only he will go and get it. Although neither of the other stories means much to Milkman at first, the story about the gold begins to represent a way out of a community that makes it difficult for him "to make up his mind whether to go forward or to turn back" (70). Moreover, as he attempts to analyze all he has been told, he realizes that "above all he wanted to escape what he knew, escape the implications of what he had been told. And all he knew in the world about the world was what other people told him" (120). The task that Milkman faces, however, is not to escape the various versions of the past that are told to him but to piece them together into his own coherent version. Only after he undertakes his own personal quest for knowledge is he able to do so.

The story Ruth tells him is another version of a story he has already been told—the story of her relationship with her father, Dr. Foster, and of her marriage to Macon. According to her version, Macon deliberately killed her father by withholding his medicine. She denies any perversity about her actions concerning her father's death and informs Milkman that it is only because of Pilate that she or he is alive. That she tells her version of the past only after he discovers her visiting her father's grave is a sign that her story, like Macon's, is motivated by guilt-ridden self-interest. Convinced that Macon has made him believe she is "a silly, self-ish, queer, faintly obscene woman" (123), she attempts to alter her son's image of her. What she does, however, is to confirm his suspicions that his family is abnormal and that the past as a coherent story is inaccessible to him.

Aside from Pilate, there is one other person whose stories are not motivated by self-interest, and that is Milkman's best friend, Guitar Bains. Street-wise and political, proud and sensitive, he attempts to tell Milkman the story of the Seven Days to inspire him to political action as well as to enlighten him about racial and social realities. Guitar attempts to teach him how to survive in their community and how to perceive the world as a whole. As a member of the gang Seven Days and as Milkman's confidant and friend, Guitar becomes his most regular contact with the community outside of his sterile, money- and status-conscious family. When Macon's story upsets Milkman, he searches for Guitar, whom he considers "the one person whose clarity never failed him" (79). He finds him in Tommy's Barbershop in the middle of a loud discussion with some other men about the Emmett Till murder. The significance of this scene is that it provides Morrison with a useful narrative strategy for bearing witness to the oral tradition of men's verbal rituals, to Milkman's precarious status of being in the community but not of it, and to the means by which black males become socialized into African-American life and culture.

At the beginning of the scene, Milkman "trie[s] to focus on the crisscrossed conversations" (80) of the men. The flow of the conversation goes from a disagreement about whether the newspapers will publish the story of the racial killing, to name-calling, to a commentary on what the black community's response should be. From there the conversation splinters into an array of narratives: "The men began to trade tales of atrocities, first stories they had heard, then those they'd witnessed, and finally the things that had happened to themselves. A litany of personal humiliation, outrage, and anger turned sicklelike back to themselves as humor. They laughed then, uproariously, about the speed with which they had run, the pose they had assumed, the ruse they had invented to escape or decrease some threat to their manliness, their humanness" (83). Although Guitar is an integral part and eager participant in this narrative ritual, Milkman remains noticeably silent. His silence thus reiterates his alienation not only from his family but from his peers and his community. While the community's sense of self is affirmed, Milkman's lack of a sense of self comes into sharper focus.

When Milkman attempts to share his mixed emotions about his father's story with Guitar, Guitar advises him to "forget it" and to realize that "people do funny things. Specially us. The cards are stacked against us and just trying to stay in the game, stay alive and in the game, makes us do funny things. Things we can't help. Things that make us hurt one another" (87).

Later, when Milkman senses that their friendship is weakening under the strain of Guitar's involvement with the Seven Days, he confronts Guitar with a barrage of questions about the group and its purpose. Guitar responds: "There is a society . . . made up of a few men who are willing to take some risks. They don't initiate anything; they don't even choose. They are as indifferent as rain. But when a Negro child, Negro woman, or Negro man is killed by whites and nothing is done about it by *their* law and *their* courts, this society selects a similar victim at random and they execute him or her in a similar manner if they can" (154). Recognizing the ultimate risk involved, Guitar adds: "If I'm caught, I'll just die earlier than I'm supposed to. And how I die or when doesn't interest me. What I die *for* does. It's the same as what I live for. . . . It's not about . . . living longer. It's about how you live and why" (159–60).

Guitar's account of the gang and his life calls attention to the lack of focus and purpose that characterizes Milkman's life. Even though Milkman considers his friend's vision as one of martyr-dom gone awry, he nevertheless envies Guitar's willingness to take risks. He begins to feel that Guitar's assessment of him—that "if things ever got tough [he'd] melt" and that he was "not a se-rious person" (104)—was accurate. All of his relationships and interactions with others convince him that "his life was pointless, aimless, and . . . that he didn't concern himself an awful lot about other people" (107). It is not until he takes the risks of venturing from his home and searching for his heritage that he attains the selfless love he admires and the sense of direction he craves.

Ultimately, it is Pilate's story that proves the most valuable to Milkman. Though Macon warns Milkman to stay away from the eccentric old herbalist, shaman, conjure woman, and bootlegger, she nevertheless remains his teacher and spiritual guide. Described as a "natural healer" (150) who came "struggling out of the womb without help from throbbing muscles or the pressure of swift womb water . . . [with] a . . . stomach [that] was . . . at no place interrupted by a navel" (27), Pilate embodies the folk aesthetic and mythic impulse all in one. On one hand, living in a darkened house surrounded by trees, practicing witchcraft and healing and making wine, she is very much rooted in the landscape. On the other, the opinion of women in the community that she is "some-thing that God never made" (144), coupled with her claim to have "spoken often to the dead" (149), give her a mythical, other-worldly quality. Recognizing that many in the community regard her as a freak because she has no navel, she decides it would be best if "she threw away every assumption she had learned and began at zero" (149). She essentially deconstructs herself, and from that point on[34] "her alien's compassion for troubled people ripened her and—the consequence of the knowledge she had made up or acquired—kept her just barely within the boundaries of the elaborately socialized world of people. Her dress might

---

34. Tate, "Toni Morrison," in *Black Women Writers,* ed. Tate, 125–26.

be outrageous to them, but her respect for other people's privacy—which they were all intense about—was balancing" (149). Thus it is apt that Pilate is the storyteller who will guide Milkman to the true story of his ancestors, for, like him, she is in the community, accepted by it, but not really of it.

Like Mrs. Todd in *Pointed Firs,* Pilate is a Demeter figure. She presides over her own backwoods corner of the world, possesses mystical powers, and engages in the arts of root working and herbal healing. Because she assumes a maternal role by "mothering" Milkman with spiritual nurturance and by offering him a haven from his "dead" household, she resembles Demeter, who assumes a maternal role by nursing Demophoon, the son of Metaneira. As a member of a three-woman household, she reminds us that Demeter was also part of the familiar triad of maiden, nymph, and crone, feminine terms that correspond to Hagar, Reba, and Pilate, respectively, and that evoke female stages of life and feminine alternatives to male power and ways of knowing.[35] Moreover, Pilate's sad wandering from place to place, collecting a rock from each stop on her lonely journey across the country, corresponds to Demeter's wandering search for Persephone that accounts for seasonal changes on earth. Finally, just as the Greek goddess Demeter is believed to mediate between earth and the underworld, Pilate mediates between this world and the next, engaging in the life-giving arts of herbal medicine on one hand and communicating with and carrying the bones of her deceased father on the other. Thus she mediates between the present and the past.

Ironically, the version of the past that Pilate shares with Milkman is a web of misinterpretations, misinformation, and misnaming. Yet because Pilate is the "woman who had as much to do with his future as she had his past" (36), Milkman discerns the genuine compassion that suffuses her memories of the past, in contrast to the guilt and bitterness that seethe through the stories

35. See Graves, *Greek Myths,* I, 95.

his parents tell. The first and most important story that Pilate tells is the one embedded in the song she sings so often, sometimes alone, sometimes in chorus with Reba and Hagar. The song exemplifies Morrison's folk aesthetic through its "blues beat," and it exemplifies her mythic impulse through its "choral note."[36] In its ability to transfix Milkman and Guitar when they sneak over to Pilate's house, the song elicits a response that Morrison claims is characteristic of the African-American oral tradition.[37] The song has a similar effect on Macon when he overhears the three women singing it one night as he strolls by Pilate's house. Milkman is able to solve the riddle hidden within the song only at the end of his quest for self-knowledge. In the narrative framing that is signified by the song in Pilate's story, which has within it the story of Pilate's grandfather as well as the story of an entire race, Morrison skillfully suggests the intricate, complex, and often inaccessible nature of the past as a network of narratives.

The rest of Pilate's story is full of misinterpretations and misinformation, but they are revealed as such only when Milkman completes his quest. It is only at the end of his quest that he realizes Pilate was not carrying the bones of the white man Macon killed in self-defense but the bones of her own father. It is also at the end that he realizes their father's ghost does not tell Pilate to sing, but it calls the name of his mother, Sing, short for the Indian name Singing Bird. It is, finally, only at the end that Milkman learns that the original song contained the name of his great-grandfather—Solomon. But before Milkman begins his quest he must undergo a few additional preparatory experiences. The most important of these are getting free from Hagar and attempting to steal the gold his father convinces him Pilate had stolen from him.

In the early days of his relationship with Hagar, he assumes he is deeply in love with her, but when Guitar introduces him to other girls, he realizes the puppy-love nature of their relationship.

36. See McCluskey, "Conversation with Toni Morrison," 82–88, and Morrison, "Rootedness," 341.
37. Morrison, "Rootedness," 341.

When he tries to withdraw from it, she becomes more possessive, a turn of events that causes him to describe her as the "third beer . . . the one you drink because it's there, because it can't hurt, and because what difference does it make" (91). Later, when he does sever the relationship, Hagar begins a monthly ritual of trying to kill him. Morrison clearly depicts Hagar's obsession as a tragic flaw, yet once again she also depicts Milkman's inability to sustain a relationship with another human being.

When Milkman realizes he has "stretched his carefree boyhood out for thirty-one years" (98), which is long enough, he decides he wants to be on his own. In sharing his desire with Macon he inadvertently mentions the sack Pilate calls her "inheritance" (163). Macon's assumption that this is the sack of gold he had long wondered about motivates him to beg Milkman to get it. Not yet ready to take a risk on his own, Milkman solicits the help of Guitar, who "could still create the sense of danger and life lived on the cutting edge" (177). As they make plans to steal the sack from Pilate's house, they observe a peacock making a series of attempts to fly. When Milkman inquires why flight is so difficult for this particular bird, Guitar responds: "Too much tail. All that jewelry weighs it down. Like vanity can't nobody fly with all that shit. Wanna fly, you got to give up the shit that weighs you down" (179). The scene is important not only because of its prophetic implications but because the sight of the bird inspires Milkman's reveries of freedom.

He admits to himself that, unlike Guitar, he does not want the money per se but to escape the feeling of being "off center": "He just wanted to beat a path away from his parents' past, which was also their present which was threatening to become his present as well. . . . He wanted to know as little as possible" (180). Thus he cannot get excited about the promise of gold. He considers his father's long story a "Jack and the Beanstalk . . . fairy tale mess" (183). But because "Guitar believed it, gave it a crisp concreteness, and . . . made it into an act, an important, real and daring thing to do," he decides to go along: "He felt a self inside himself emerge, a clean-lined definite self. A self that could join the chorus at Railroad Tommy's with more than laughter. He could tell this" (184). He decides to respond to "the clarion call in Guitar's voice" (183) to live his life.

The significance of this decision is that even though he fails to find gold in Pilate's sack, he gains an opportunity to learn her version of how the bones came into her possession. She claims that her father came to her in death and told her she "just can't fly on off and leave a body. . . . A human life is precious" (208). This message prompted her to return to the cave to secure the bones of the man Macon had murdered in self-defense. Pilate's telling becomes information Milkman will use on his journey to the South allegedly in search of gold but actually in search of his identity.

The events of Part I lead to Guitar's call for Milkman to make the necessary journey to his own life. From his unusual birth, to his altercation with his father, to his confrontation with his mother, to his severance from Hagar and education from Pilate, every experience in his community prepares him for the quest. All these experiences put the journey from the city to the country, from the North to the South, in perspective. Morrison establishes the community as the text that Milkman must read, reject, and then re-read if he is to make meaning of his life. He can integrate the versions of the past into a coherent story only when he takes the necessary risk to live his life on his own.

In Part II of *Song of Solomon*, Morrison again uses the folk aesthetic, but she consciously combines it with her mythic impulse to give structure to the narrative and to suggest the traditional rite of passage of the mythic hero. To appreciate the journey that Milkman undertakes, we should review the essential phases of the mythic quest.

In *The Hero with a Thousand Faces*, Joseph Campbell explains that the "standard path of the mythological adventure is represented in the rites of passage: separation, initiation and return."[38]

38. Campbell, *Hero with a Thousand Faces*, 30.

Although Morrison expands on this monomyth to include allusions to African-American myth, Greek myth, the Bible, and folk and fairy tales, Campbell's paradigm can be used to analyze Milkman's journey from North to South. Because Morrison uses a mythopoeic process that precludes a complete reliance on this paradigm, it can be expanded to include the following words, which correspond more closely to her narrative intent and design: birth and youth, alienation, quest, confrontation, and reintegration.[39] Although the quest itself takes precedence in much male fiction, Morrison's concern with the community and the self, the "nest" and the journey, dictates the disproportionate amount of time and space she devotes to the phases of birth, youth, and alienation in Part I to establish the context for the quest, to explain the "how come and why" of her "way-out tale" (76).[40]

Milkman's quest begins with his separation from his urban community in Michigan and his initiation into the rural landscape, first of Pennsylvania, then of Virginia. When he arrives in Danville, Pennsylvania, he recalls the fairy tale of Hansel and Gretel. The allusion to this narrative in the text serves to comment on the illusory nature of his quest for gold and to foreshadow the dangers that await him. His reflections on the airplane, however, are of his lifelong preoccupation with flying. He reflects on how the plane ride "exhilarated him, encouraged illusion and a feeling of invulnerability. High above the clouds, heavy yet light, caught in the stillness of speed . . . sitting in intricate metal become glistening bird, it was not possible to believe he had ever made a mistake, or could. . . . This one time he wanted to go solo. In the air, away from real life, he felt free, but on the ground, when he talked to Guitar just before he left, the wings of all those other people's nightmares flapped in his face and constrained him" (220). Despite the brief reference to the home he has fled, his reflections on flying foreshadow the freedom that awaits him.

39. Harry Slochower, *Mythopoesis: Mythic Patterns in the Literary Classics* (Detroit, 1970), 23–26. Also see Lee, *"Song of Solomon."*
40. Tate, "Toni Morrison," in *Black Women Writers,* ed. Tate, 122.

The first person he attempts to find is Circe. The resonances from Greek myth in her name are ironic at the same time that they suggest Morrison's conscious use of Homeric parallels.[41] It can be argued that the plethora of classical allusions are an example of her desire to "provide the places and spaces so that the reader can participate."[42] The temptation throughout the entire novel, but especially in Part II, is to make a series of one-to-one correspondences between her text and classical texts. But in the irony, complexity, and multiplicity of mythopoesis, this temptation is thwarted and the reader must acknowledge a variety of ways to interpret the names, to read the signs, to understand the rituals. Thus the reader is constantly in a situation that is analogous to Milkman's.

When Milkman asks for Circe on his arrival in Danville, he meets people who not only know Circe and where she lives but who know his father and aunt. Reverend Cooper thus welcomes Milkman with a greeting that is familiar in African-American culture, especially in the South—"I know your people" (229), a phrase that signifies not just a knowledge of a few names but an ability to make genealogical connections, to tell stories that reveal family history, and to establish the basis for conversation and acceptance. Thus this greeting signifies the folk aesthetic of storytelling that punctuates the narrative.

When Milkman begins to explain how he got there and found Reverend Cooper, he can tell by the minister's desire to get all the facts straight that he was "already . . . framing the story for his friends" (230). As a guest at the minister's house, Milkman gets "long visits from every old man in the town who remembered his father or grandfather" (234). The verbal exchange between Milk-

41. Morrison admits that the "Ulysses theme, the leaving home" theme has a strong appeal for her. She explains that the "tragic direction of her work could be a consequence of her being a classics minor. See Stepto, "Intimate Things in Place," in *Chant of Saints,* ed. Harper and Stepto, 226, and Le Clair, "Language Must Not Sweat," 28.

42. Morrison, "Rootedness," 341.

man and these elders of the community who knew his ancestors not only illustrates the oral tradition in process but suggests Milkman's naive, uninitiated status. Unlike the older men at home who looked upon him with scorn as the son of a slum landlord, however, these men have the utmost respect for Macon, whom they remember through Milkman's grandfather, whose farm was the envy of everyone. Thus, in this setting, Milkman enjoys privileged status—the men literally pay homage to him.

He notices how the men talk on and on, using him as the "ignition . . . [for] their memories" of Macon as "the farmer they wanted to be" (235). Milkman attempts to join their conversation by "rattling off assets" (236), the accomplishments of Macon II, his father. This scene serves as counterpoint to the barbershop scene at home, where he felt isolated; yet in this setting closer to his real "home"—the South—he feels comfortable enough to participate in the verbal ritual. The irony of his participation is that it is based on a false sense of pride, on ownership of things beyond self-knowledge. Thus the scene suggests how Milkman is already being transformed, but it also reveals that he is still a long way from being his own person as well as a genuine heir. To complete this transformation, he must undergo not verbal rituals but real risk-taking, life-threatening rituals in the tradition of the mythic hero. These rituals take the form of a meeting with Circe, a journey to the cave of his ancestors, a verbal battle that becomes a physical challenge, a hunt, and a threat on his life from his friend turned antagonist, Guitar.

Unlike the Circe of Greek myth, who turns the men of Odysseus into swine, Circe, the midwife who brought Macon and Pilate into the world, is more like a prophetess or sibyl. Thus Morrison draws not on the image of her as a witch, an image that would have coincided with Milkman's fantasy of her from childhood, but on her image as one who points the way.[43] Moreover, Morrison revises the mythic figure of Circe and the negative ste-

---

43. Graves, *Greek Myths*, I, 115, II, 354–64.

reotype of the crone by transforming them both into a positive depiction of the crone as shaman. As Milkman listens to Circe's story of his father and aunt, he reflects on her importance to his family and realizes that, like Pilate, she is a "healer, deliverer [who] in another world would have been the head nurse at Mercy" (246). Because she directs him to the cave that once held his grandfather's remains and tells him his grandfather's real name was Jake and not Macon, she becomes a spiritual midwife to Milkman, helping him give birth to himself.

The cave that Circe directs him to is the location of his next ritual. Symbolically, this ritual is a turning point in Milkman's journey because it begins his series of encounters with lifethreatening situations. When he enters the cave, he is "blinded by the absence of light" (251). This suggests the descent of the mythic hero into darkness or hell prior to his reintegration into the community. In Milkman's case, however, such a descent is premature. It can be argued that this blindness recalls Tiresias, the seer and reader of signs whose loss of sight is compensated by an ability to see inward. Because Milkman's loss of sight is temporary, it foreshadows or at least parallels his journey from ignorance to self-knowledge. When he leaves the cave, his excessive hunger prompts him to eat leaves. He has lost his watch and must tell time by looking at the sun. In a sense, then, his journey to the cave represents a shedding of old ways of seeing and a return to a primordial state of innocence. Having descended into the pit of the cave (a symbolic death before rebirth), he finds not only that it does not contain gold, but that it contains "nothing at all" (252). Like Tiresias, however, who gains greater insight to compensate for his loss of eyesight and who becomes a reader of signs, Milkman gains from his journey the discovery that his "mind began to function clearly" (259). He realizes then that he must leave Danville, a way station between the past and the future, and head for Virginia, his ancestral home.

Once Milkman arrives in Virginia, the narrative movement seems to fit the image that Morrison uses to describe it—"the image . . . of a train picking up speed."[44] Her choice of this image captures the intense speed with which events occur near the end of the novel. Almost from the moment he gets to Shalimar, Virginia, he realizes that it is a very different milieu from Danville. The hostility he begins to feel corresponds to the change from the quest phase of his journey into the phase of confrontations in which the mythic hero must undergo rites of passage or life-crisis trials.[45] This change in turn corresponds to the shift in his motivations after leaving the cave. Milkman's quest for gold turns into a quest for his family history. With these changes, Milkman's journey becomes more and more dangerous with each confrontation.

The first sign of danger comes in the form of the news that Guitar has been in town already, is looking for him, and has left a message that Milkman's "day has come" (262). Milkman recognizes the encoded death threat of the Seven Days but cannot figure out why Guitar would leave such a message. He does not worry about it long because a more immediate threat confronts him. What begins as a request for information becomes a life-and-death threat he cannot ignore. When he asks when repair work on his car might be completed, he unwittingly adds that if it cannot be finished in time, he may have to buy a new car. He is unaware of the implicit insult in his announcement. It immediately sets him apart, alienates him, and calls attention to his money, his city clothes, and his northern accent. To the group of men standing around Solomon's General Store, these are reminders of their status relative to his. That he does not bother "to know their names, and believed himself too good to tell them his" (266), irritates them into initiating the name-calling verbal battle known as "the dozens" in African-American culture.[46] The anger escalates into a brawl with knives and broken bottles that ends only when two women enter the store.

The next ritual Milkman must undergo is the hunt. Four older

44. Tate, "Toni Morrison," in *Black Women Writers,* ed. Tate, 124.
45. Lee, *"Song of Solomon,"* 69.
46. Le Clair, "Language Must Not Sweat," 27.

men, who witness his survival of the confrontation with the younger men, invite him to join them on a bobcat hunt: "It was as though now that the young men had had their chance, with unsatisfactory results, the older men would take over. Their style, of course would be different. No name-calling toilet contest for them. No knives either, or hot breath and knotted neck muscles. They would test him, match and beat him, probably on some other ground" (269).

The ritual of the hunt recalls the Cyclops episode in the *Odyssey*. The "monster" Milkman faces, however, presents both a psychological and a real threat. As a rite of passage into manhood, therefore, the hunt becomes his most dangerous encounter. Although "he [has] never handled a firearm in his life," he accepts the challenge because "he had stopped evading things, sliding through, over, and around difficulties" (271). Yet he cannot understand why there were "all these people roaming the world trying to kill him. . . . He had thought this place, this Shalimar, was going to be home. His original home. His people came from here, his grandfather and grandmother. All the way down South people had been nice to him, generous, helpful. In Danville they had made him the object of hero worship. In his own home town his name spelled dread and grudging respect. But here, in his 'home,' he was unknown, unloved, and damn near killed" (270). In his not yet fully initiated state he does not realize that Shalimar will be his "home" only when he sheds his ego, participates in the rites of passage, and proves himself to be a member of the community. Shalimar cannot be his home, that is, until he sheds romanticized notions of place and makes the emotional investment necessary to relinquish the vestiges of status and privilege that separate him from his people. His decision to accompany Calvin Breakstone, Luther Solomon, Small Boy, and Omar on the hunt begins this phase of his initiation process.

The hunt tests more than his skill with a shotgun, however. It tests his ability to trust nature and his instincts, to endure bodily discomfort, to defend himself, and to participate in a shared struggle with a common goal—it tests his ability to take risks and survive. It is on the hunt that he experiences his most existential moment:

> Under the moon, on the ground, alone . . . his self—the cocoon that was "personality"—gave way. He could barely see his own hand, and couldn't see his feet. . . . Thoughts came, unobstructed by other people, by things, even by the sight of himself. There was nothing here to help him—not his money, his car, his father's reputation, his suit, or his shoes. In fact they hampered him. . . . All he had started out with on his journey was gone. . . . [They] would be of no help out here, where all a man had was what he was born with, or had learned to use. And endurance. Eyes, ears, nose, taste, touch—and some other sense that he knew he did not have: an ability to separate out, of all the things there were to sense, the one that life itself might depend on. (277)

This moment of introspection recalls Guitar's comment on the male peacock's inability to fly because of all the "shit that weighs [it] down" (179). Freed from these encumbrances, Milkman learns to listen to the earth and to detect his friend Guitar lurking in the woods waiting to kill him. Thus he is not only the hunter but the hunted. Yet he succeeds in defending himself against Guitar's attack, he attains a sense of direction through the woods, and he admits to the group that he had been "scared to death" (280). The irony is that his old self *does* die, for at the end of the hunt he finds himself "exhilarated by simply walking the earth. Walking it like he belonged on it; like his legs were stalks, tree trunks, a part of his body that extended down down down into the rock and the soil, and were comfortable there—on the earth and on the place where he walked. And he did not limp" (281). The reference to the limp skillfully signifies that the rites of passage are over. He has passed over into manhood and is therefore ready for the final phase of the quest, reintegration or return.

There are several parts to the last phase. First he spends time with a prostitute named Sweet, who is a kind of Calypso figure.

Even though his time spent with her is totally sensuous and ful-filling, it detains him from finding Guitar and from continuing his search for the pieces to the story of his past. Yet the satisfying nature of their lovemaking, Milkman's offer to bathe her, and the chores they share all reveal that the ability to reciprocate love has replaced selfish indifference. From Sweet's he journeys to the home of Susan Byrd, who fills in additional pieces of his family's story. He realizes that he does not feel close to her and her sister, but he does "feel connected, as though there was some cord or pulse or information they shared" (293). Again, although she does not fill in all the pieces at once, she represents the emphasis on connections that begins to characterize the transformed Milkman. When he finally meets up with Guitar, his friend-turned-enemy greets him with "My man" (295), a greeting replete with irony, for he has severed the friendship through his attempt to kill Milk-man. It also acknowledges his changed character from boylike na-ïveté to mature manhood. Yet the greeting also points to Guitar's desire to possess his life, that he still wants to murder him because he believes Milkman has deceived him about the gold. When they separate, each realizes the tenuous nature of their friendship.

Throughout his stay in Shalimar, pronounced *"Shalleemone"* (261), Milkman hears children singing. When he first arrives, he describes it as a "kind of ring-around-the-rosy or Little Sally Walker game" (264). He considers the verse a meaningless rhyme:

Jay the only son of Solomon
Come booba yalle, come booba tambee
Whirled about and touch the sun
Come booba yalle, come booba tambee . . . (264)

It reminds him that his own childhood was bereft of opportunities to be with other children or to "play circle games . . . singing games" (264). Once he is initiated, he does not hear it as a nursery rhyme but as the "old blues song Pilate sang all the time" (300). He notices that the words are slightly different. Rather than "Su-garman," they sing the name "Solomon." In remembering Pilate, he begins to make another connection beyond himself, remembering not only Pilate but his parents and even Hagar. In a highly introspective moment he realizes "he was homesick . . . for the very people he had been hell-bent to leave. His mother's quiet, crooked, apologetic smile . . . his father. An old man now, who acquired things and used people to acquire more things. As the son of Macon Dead the first, he paid homage to his own father's life and death by loving what that father had loved: property . . . the bountifulness of life. He loved these things to excess because he loved his father to excess. Owning, building, acquiring— that was his life, his future, his present, and all the history he knew. . . . His mind turned to Hagar and how he had treated her. . . . He had used her" (300–301).

When he comes out of his reverie, the children are still singing. For the first time, however, he connects parts of the song to fragments and experiences. Ironically, when he decides to write the words down, he has no pen or pencil and nothing to write on but his airplane ticket stub. He thus is left with no choice but to listen and memorize it. The song is described in terms we associate with ritual—"repeat," "rhythmic," "rhyming action game," "performed the round over and over" (303). At this point, Morrison inserts the entire text of the song into the narrative, thereby signifying Milkman's transformed consciousness. He no longer hears merely a verse or a chorus but the entire song, the complete tale within the song:

> Jake the only son of Solomon
> Come booba yalle, come booba tambee
> Whirled about and touched the sun
> Come konka yalle, come konka tambee
>
> Left that baby in a white man's house
> Come booba yalle, come booba tambee
> Heddy took him to a red man's house
> Come konka yalle, come konka tambee

Black lady fell down on the ground
Come booba yalle, come booba tambee
Threw her body all around
Come konka yalle, come konka tambee

Solomon and Ryna Belali Shalut
Yaruba Medina Muhammet too
Nestor Kalina Saraka cake
Twenty-one children, the last one Jake!

O Solomon don't leave me here
Cotton balls to choke me
O Solomon don't leave me here
Buckra's arms to yoke me

Solomon done fly, Solomon done gone
Solomon cut across the sky, Solomon gone home. (303)

As a performed ritual, the song signals a cathartic epiphany for
Milkman.

The significance of the song is threefold: for Milkman, it signals the story of his family; for the community Shalimar, it functions as a kind of cultural glue through the children who learn,
sing, and perform it; and for the reader, it serves as an illustration
of Morrison's folk aesthetic and mythic impulse at work. The
song tells the story of Solomon, an African slave, who, one day
in the middle of work in the cotton field, decides he will tolerate
his oppression no longer. He flies away home, back to Africa,
leaving his wife, Ryna, and twenty children. He tries to take his
youngest child, Jake, with him, but drops him soon after he gets
in the air. For Milkman, the children are no longer singing a nonsense rhyme. He realizes, as he recognizes names Circe had mentioned, that "these children were singing a story about his own
people!" (304).

That Milkman learns the song from a group of children suggests the cultural function of the folktale. It gives cohesion to the community in that the children learn, sing, and perform it in an almost ritualistic fashion. Thus it is a conduit for history and culture even though to them it is merely a nonsense rhyme. For the reader, the song serves another function. It illustrates and thus affirms Morrison's folk aesthetic and mythic impulse as dynamic communal processes that could link the self to its community. The song is a folk narrative that confirms the mythic hero at the same time that it affirms the identity of the hero who hears it. Thus it illustrates the ability of narrative to transform consciousness.

In the narrative within the "song of Solomon," Morrison consciously draws on the motif of flying that is endemic to the African-American folk and literary tradition.[47] She has stated that "people who could fly . . . was [sic] always part of the folklore of my life; flying was one of our gifts."[48] It is safe to assume, then, that the song upon which she bases her novel is a variant of the well-known Gullah folktale, a variant which Susan L. Blake argues is the least common of the possible twenty-seven reported in *Drums and Shadows*.[49] In selecting the variant in which an indi-

47. The flying motif is common in the African-American literary tradition. Morrison continues the tradition at the same time that she revises it. For discussions of this tradition as it relates to her novel, see Bruck, "Returning to One's Roots," in *Afro-American Novel,* ed. Bruck and Karren; Hovet and Lounsberry, "Flying as Symbol"; and Lee, *"Song of Solomon."*

48. Le Clair, "Language Must Not Sweat," 26–27; Ruas, *Conversations with American Writers,* 241.

49. Blake points out that Morrison chose the least common variant of this folktale, thus changing its emphasis. There are twenty-seven variants. In twenty-two of them, the flying Africans are a group, in three they are a couple, and in only two, an individual. In Morrison's novel, according to Blake, the emphasis is not on where he is going, but on whom he left. I disagree that this is the effect of the changed emphasis because in the novel, Milkman flies in the direction of Guitar, toward him in fact. Morrison's emphasis is on Africa as home—on the return home. See Blake, "Folklore and Community in *Song of Solomon,*" *MELUS,* VII (Fall, 1980), 77–82, and Georgia Writers Project, *Drums and Shadows* (Athens, Ga., 1940).

vidual rather than a group takes flight, however, Morrison is not only using mythopoeic license, but she is also attempting to re-iterate the dual theme of the individual quest and affirmation of the community. In other words, though the tale focuses on the flight of one, the narration of it serves a cultural function for the community that parallels if not supersedes the focus on the individual. Morrison's choice of this variant enables her to use it as a cautionary tale to evoke and revise the "culturally monolithic standard" of the "monolithic self" that Sandra A. Zagarell argues is pervasive in Western culture.[50]

Realizing he has nearly all the pieces to his story, Milkman returns to Susan Byrd for help in completing it. At her home he not only confirms the connections he has made but learns that Jake, his grandfather, "was one of those flying African children" (321) and that the flying African was named Solomon. Susan then helps him connect the remaining fragments of his ancestry: "She talked on and on while Milkman sat back and listened to gossip, stories, legends, speculations. His mind was ahead of hers, behind hers, with hers, and bit by bit, with what she said, what he knew, what he guessed, he put it all together" (323). Connecting all the names, Milkman learns that when Solomon dropped Jake, his wife, Ryna, went insane and died. An Indian named Heddy found Jake and raised him along with her own daughter, Singing Bird. Sing and Jake ran away together to the North and got married. When they registered at the Freedman's Bureau en route to Pennsylvania, Sing persuaded Jake to keep the misname Macon Dead so as to erase his slavery past. They have two children, Macon and Pilate. Sing died while giving birth to Pilate. When a white man killed Jake over his farm, Circe cared for Macon and Pilate until they decided that they wanted to be on their own. Macon headed north, married Ruth, and had three children. Pilate traveled around but eventually settled in the same community.

50. Sandra A. Zagarell, "Narrative of Community: The Identification of a Genre," *Signs,* XIII (1988), 504.

Having listened to the complete narrative of his ancestors, he is able to connect the past with the present, to see himself in context. In his great-grandfather, however, he sees not just an ancestor but a hero. As he exclaims to Sweet: "He could fly! You hear me? My great-granddaddy could fly! Goddam!" (328). Empowered by the story of his heritage and the attendant self-knowledge, he finally returns home. But his return is brief and purposeful. He returns home to share his story with Pilate and to take her back to the South to give her father a proper burial. Milkman's story helps her revise her misinformation and celebrate the past she has already shared with him. As they ride back to Shalimar, the utter contentment she feels is reflected in the words "peace circled her" (334), which both describe and foreshadow the fateful outcome of her return.

When Milkman arrives in Shalimar with Pilate, there is "general merriment at his quick return and Pilate blended into the population like a stick of butter in a churn" (335). It is clear that he is returning as a hero and that Morrison is bringing the identification between him and his ancestor into sharper focus. Milkman accompanies Pilate to Solomon's Leap, the ridge from which Solomon took flight, where they bury her father's bones. Pilate then removes the earring that contains her name—the only word her father ever wrote—and places it atop the small grave. Within seconds she is shot by Guitar, who has hidden among the rocks hoping to shoot Milkman. As she lies dying in his arms, she asks him to sing. Knowing no songs but the song of Solomon, he sings it to her. Having learned the story of his past, his family, and himself, he can sing in affirmation of his reconnection with her, his spiritual mother and griot, whose song contained the only story he could really use.[51] Contrary to what Macon believed, Pilate had given him something he could use in *this* world as well as the next. When she dies, two birds circle over her, and he realizes that he loved her because she had taught him that "without ever leaving the ground she could fly" (336).

51. See Skerrett, "Recitation to the Griot," 201.

As he stands up, he tells Guitar that if he wants his life, "Here I am" (337). The echoing rocks that reverberate his words signify the affirmation of self that characterizes the end of his quest. The final words of the text suggest that he then makes the final connection that remains to be made—the affirmation of his community, symbolized in Guitar, his spiritual brother: "Without wiping away the tears, taking a deep breath, or even bending his knees— he leaped. As fleet and bright as lodestar he wheeled toward Guitar and it did not matter which one of them would give up his ghost in the killing arms of his brother. For he knew what Shalimar knew: If you surrendered to the air, you could *ride* it" (337). The conclusion represents a reconciliation between past and present, the community and the self. Milkman has come full circle from being born on the day after a tragic Icarus-like flight to a triumphant flight of his own in the tradition of his African ancestor. He has plunged back into the past, recovered his name, and gained the knowledge necessary to tell a coherent story of his own life. He has learned how to read and reread the past to make meaning of his life and to affirm his place in time and space. His life bears witness to the novel's epigraph: "The fathers may soar / And the children may know their names." Bearing witness is the narrative process that the novel validates.

Toni Morrison attempts to bear witness to knowledge, language, traditions, and stories that her people have forgotten or that others have discredited. She suggests to her community of readers that they must take a journey like Milkman's into the cultural roots of the past if the present is to become meaningful to them.[52] The journey is thus a flight and a return, a flight from the

52. The phrase *community of readers* is one I borrow from another scholar. See Kathleen O'Shaughnessy, " 'Life life life life': The Community as Chorus in *Song of Solomon*," in *Critical Essays on Toni Morrison*, ed. Nellie McKay (Boston, 1988), 126. Although they are beyond the scope of this study, Morrison's recent comments on the African roots of Western civilization and the work of Martin Bernal are indicative of how some of the distinctions between African and Greek mythology must be historicized and deconstructed if we are to gain a better understanding of our past. See Morrison, "Unspeakable Things Unspoken"; and Martin

present to the past to return to the present. As Paul Ricoeur states, "The hero *is* who he *was*."[53] The narrative circle of Toni Morrison contains a nexus of myth and folklore, magic and realism that at once draws on narratives from Greek mythology, African myth, African-American folklore, and fairy tales. In making the flying African tale the focus of her novel, she subverts the temptation to read strict Homeric parallels into her narrative or to repeat the tradition of flight as escape. Her folk aesthetic gives substance to her novel, while the mythic impulse gives it form. She uses the narrative tradition in chorus through mythopoesis to create her own myth of affirmation and triumph. Even though the temptation is to rely on one narrative paradigm, she continually reminds her readers of the multiplicity of meaning and the possibility and freedom to name, unname, and rename to shape our own experiences.

Yet Morrison does not keep the emphasis on the individual quest or the individual self in the tradition of male writers. Milkman's consciousness is transformed only when he moves outside himself and listens to and participates in the narratives of his family and his community. Until he engages in this process, he lives under the same illusion of self-sufficiency that dehumanizes his father and that blinds both men to the chain of interdependence that connects them to others. As Jessica Benjamin argues, it is the denial of interdependence that not only perpetuates male domination and the illusion of freedom but also prohibits the very journey to self-knowledge they attempt to make.[54] Indeed, like Sarah Orne Jewett, Morrison suggests that the better part of the journey is not to the self but to the community of others. Though Milkman's flight is in recognition of his own

Bernal, *The Fabrication of Ancient Greece, 1785–1985,* Vol. I of *Black Athena: The Afroasiatic Roots of Classical Civilization* (New Brunswick, 1987).

53. Paul Ricoeur, "Narrative Time," in *On Narrative,* ed. W. J. T. Mitchell (Chicago, 1981), 182.

54. Benjamin, *Bonds of Love,* 185–98.

power, the transformation of his consciousness is an affirmation of the past and community he has come to understand, respect, and love. The achievement of *Song of Solomon* is that through the network of narrative that transforms Milkman, Toni Morrison takes on the role of griot and tells how we, her community of readers, could be transformed not only by the song in the story but by the story in the song.

4

NARRATIVE DILEMMA: JADINE AS CULTURAL ORPHAN IN *TAR BABY*

> Not to know is bad; not to wish to know is worse.
> —African proverb

> Form does not suppress . . . meaning, it only impoverishes it, it puts it at a distance, it holds it at one's disposal.
> —Roland Barthes, *Mythologies*

> For the ancestor is not only wise, he or she values racial connection, racial memory over individual fulfillment.
> —Toni Morrison

Of Toni Morrison's first four novels, *Tar Baby* (1981) is the most problematic because in it she attempts two narrative strategies—situating the central plot within an insular setting beyond the familiar geographical boundaries of the United States mainland and juxtaposing black and white characters to dramatize the racial complexities that determine the American cultural landscape.[1] Although dislocation and cross-cultural relationships figure strongly in the novel, the characterization of Jadine draws attention to a more fundamental narrative problem than either of these strategies might suggest. On one hand, Morrison wants to affirm the self-reliance and freedom of a black woman who makes choices for her life on her own terms. On the other hand, she also seeks to "point out the dangers . . . that can happen to the totally self-

---

1. Toni Morrison, *Tar Baby* (New York, 1981). Subsequent references to this novel are given parenthetically in the text. An earlier version of this chapter was published as an article, Marilyn E. Mobley, "Narrative Dilemma: Jadine as Cultural Orphan in Toni Morrison's *Tar Baby*," *Southern Review*, XXIII (1987), 761–70.

reliant if there is no historical connection."[2] More specifically, Morrison's dilemma in *Tar Baby* is how to narrate the quest of a contemporary African-American female hero who happens to be a cultural orphan, one whose sense of self is based on a denial of her own cultural heritage and an identification with one other than her own.

Nowhere are the dynamics of Morrison's narrative dilemma more clearly articulated than in the description of Jadine as she stands in the "circle of trees" where the Caribbean island swamp literally entraps her in its black, sticky substance:

> The women hanging in the trees looked down at her . . . and stopped murmuring. They were delighted when they first saw her, thinking a runaway child had been restored to them. But looking closer they saw differently. This girl was fighting to get away from them. The women hanging from the trees were quiet now, but arrogant—mindful as they were of their value, their exceptional femaleness; knowing as they did that the first world of the world had been built with their sacred properties; that they alone could hold together the stones of pyramids and the rushes of Moses's crib; knowing their steady consistency, their pace of glaciers, their permanent embrace, they wondered at the girl's desperate struggle down below to be free, to be something other than they were. (182–83)

This passage not only expresses the problem Morrison attempts to address in writing the novel but also points to the central conflict that Jadine faces in her quest to come to terms with her identity. For Morrison, the women in the trees symbolize the women she seeks to affirm—the mothers, grandmothers, and sisters to whom she dedicates the novel. For Jadine, the women in the trees represent all the women who make her feel "lonely and inauthentic" (48). While on one level *Tar Baby* appears to be simply the story of a failed love affair between a man and a woman with

2. Morrison, "Rootedness," 344.

diametrically opposed values and life-styles, on a deeper level, the novel is about the disparity Morrison sees between the women of her remembered past and the women of the present epitomized in the character of Jadine. Consequently, the biblical epigraph to the novel, which reads, "It hath been declared . . . by them . . . of the house of Chloe, that there are contentions among you," does not simply foreshadow the conflicts that arise in the Valerian Street household. Instead, it points to the serious conflicts or "contentions" that Morrison (born Chloe Anthony Wofford) examines in the character of Jadine. Indeed, the text reveals the dilemma Morrison faced in trying to depict the potential consequences of success predicated upon disconnection from one's racial identity and cultural heritage.

In speaking of her novels, Morrison asserts that "what is left out is as important as what is there."[3] Whereas listening to the stories of his family and his community determine the shape of Milkman's quest for identity, no such stories shape Jadine's quest. Conspicuously absent from Jadine's life is the storytelling tradition that could restore her to psychic wholeness. And the novel does not provide answers to the hauntingly complex questions it raises about how a marginalized culture validates itself in the presence and under the gaze of a dominant culture. Thus Morrison's dilemma is refigured in the dilemma she creates for the reader, who must not only account for the narrative spaces in Jadine's story but must weave Jadine's story into the larger narrative of African-American history and culture that informs Morrison's narrative voice.

In her interview with Nellie McKay, Morrison explains that "the writer has to solve certain kinds of problems in writing. The way in which I handle elements within a story frame is important. . . . There is always something more interesting at stake than a clear resolution in a novel. I'm interested in survival—who survives and who does not, and why—and I would

3. *Ibid.*, 341.

like to chart a course that suggests where the dangers are and where the safety might be. I do not want to bow out with easy answers to complex questions."[4] Although these statements pertain to her work in general, they also speak to the particular unresolved conflicts in *Tar Baby*. *Tar Baby* is ultimately a problematic text for the reader because Jadine poses a narrative dilemma for which Morrison has no easy answers. Yet Morrison attempts to solve her dilemma in three ways. First, she revises the mythic quest, which she characteristically defines in masculine terms, by exploring it from a black female perspective. Second, she transforms the well-known African-American folktale of the tar baby into a modern cautionary tale. As Roger Abrahams explains, cautionary tales are "moral stories" that "illustrate how disorderly and unmannerly people act and what happens to them . . . because of their misbehavior."[5] Third, Morrison structures the novel around a series of conflicts or disruptions that dramatize the interplay between form and substance, silence and truth, nest and journey, self and other, public and private, mother and daughter.[6]

The contemporary nature of *Tar Baby,* with its critiques of everything from education to racism, indicates that Morrison was seeking in the novel to expose the historical, social, and cultural dilemmas that shape late twentieth-century life. Thus *Tar Baby* can be interpreted as a modern cautionary tale in which Morrison draws on the African-American narrative tradition to expose the pitfalls for the black woman with white middle-class aspirations and to illustrate the consequences of her social and cultural "misbehavior." Although the text illustrates these consequences by ex-

4. McKay, "Interview with Toni Morrison," 420.
5. Roger Abrahams, ed., *Afro-American Folktales: Stories from Black Traditions in the New World* (New York, 1985), 118.
6. I am partially indebted to the footnoted material in Peter B. Erickson's article on nurturance for my discussion of Morrison's personal mother-daughter perspective as revealed in interviews. See Erickson, "Images of Nurturance in Toni Morrison's *Tar Baby,*" *CLA Journal,* XXVIII (1984), 28–30. For a brief discussion of matrophobia, see Davis, "Self, Society, and Myth."

amining the tensions inherent in the binary oppositions of black and white, poor and rich, female and male, mother and daughter, African and European, African-American and American, the central reasons for Jadine's divided consciousness stem from her rejection of the cultural construction of race and mothering that are part of her African-American heritage. Jadine's quest is for psychic wholeness, but because she does not heed the cautions that come to her in various forms, she experiences a failed initiation or an aborted quest. Indeed, her quest for wholeness is unsuccessful because she accepts values and mores of white middle-class culture without question and she rejects the very cultural constructions of race and mothering that could heal and transform her consciousness.

Jadine is, by Western standards, a successful woman. That she has a Sorbonne education, a degree in art history, popular acclaim as a model, and the means to live alternately in Paris, Rome, New York, and the Caribbean attest to the description of her as one who travels in the "fast lane" (117). Thus Morrison's characterization of Jadine represents a sharp departure from her first three novels.[7] In contrast to Jadine's rootlessness, the black female protagonists of *The Bluest Eye* and *Sula* are inextricably bound to clearly drawn insular black neighborhoods in the Midwest. Despite her tendency to wander, even Pilate in *Song of Solomon* is essentially a rooted individual as suggested literally and figuratively in her roles as herbalist, healer, and conjure woman. The female characters of Morrison's first three novels seem to be drawn from her recollections of "the black community [or] neighborhood [as] this life-giving, very very strong sustenance that people got from the neighborhood. . . . Every woman on the street could raise everybody's child and tell you exactly what to do and you felt that connection with those people and they felt it with you. . . . There was something special about when she [my mother] said 'Sister' and when all those women said 'Sister.'"[8] In

7. Pearl K. Bell, "Self-Seekers," *Commentary*, LXXII (August, 1981), 56–58.
8. Stepto, "Intimate Things in Place," in *Chants of Saints,* ed. Harper and Stepto, 214.

these words, Morrison is remembering the past through women who had a sense of place, identity, and authority. In associating the past with the cultural values and traditions of women such as her mother and grandmother, she reminds us of Virginia Woolf's assertion that "we think back through our mothers if we are women."[9] By characterizing Jadine as an orphan at an early age, Morrison sets up a narrative strategy whereby she can use literal "motherlessness" (281) to give expression to the disparity she senses between her own generation and that of her mother.

But for Morrison, the word *mother* refers not simply to a biological relationship but to those women who provide the nurturing associated with mothering. Moreover, the word has a historical and cultural context. As she says, "Our history as black women is the history of women who could build a house *and* have some children, and there was no problem."[10] Thus Morrison's larger concern is one of balancing ambition and nurturing. The commencement address Morrison gave at Barnard College in 1979 contains a clear articulation of her concern that contemporary women might neglect this balance in the interest of self-fulfillment: "I am suggesting that we pay as much attention to our nurturing sensibilities as to our ambition. You are moving in the direction of freedom and the function of freedom is to free somebody else. You are moving toward self-fulfillment, and the consequences of that fulfillment should be to discover that there is something just as important as you are. . . . In your rainbow journey toward the realization of personal goals, don't make choices based only on your security and your safety. . . . Let your might and your power emanate from that place in you that is nurturing and caring."[11]

9. Virginia Woolf, *A Room of One's Own* (New York, 1929), 132.

10. Quoted in Erickson, "Images of Nurturance," 29. Also see Judith Wilson, "A Conversation with Toni Morrison," *Essence,* July, 1981, p. 84.

11. Toni Morrison, "Cinderella's Stepsisters," in *Responding to Writing: A Reader for Writers,* ed. Judith Fishman (Indianapolis, 1983), 494–97. Also see Edwin McDowell, "Behind the Best Sellers: Toni Morrison," *New York Times Book Review,* July 5, 1981, p. 18.

The double-voiced nature of this passage suggests the dilemma that Morrison faced in writing *Tar Baby*. On one hand, she speaks as a peer or "daughter" cognizant of the lure of the present; on the other, she speaks as an authority or "mother" rooted in the ancestral knowledge of the past. The use of first-person pronouns signifies her identification with the ambition of graduating women, while the shift to second person signifies a distancing from them to address them with a nurturing form of knowledge. Morrison took three and a half years to write *Tar Baby* and delivered this speech while the novel that would share its thematic thrust was in progress. *Tar Baby,* then, is a tribute to a remembered but devalued history and a cautionary tale for daughters like Jadine, who define themselves against themselves, their mothers, and their cultural history in the interest of self-fulfillment and freedom.

By focusing on mother-daughter relations, Morrison speaks through racial and gendered discourses rather than through the traditional discourse of biological family relations. Through racial discourse she foregrounds the presence of the mother as "the advising, benevolent, protective wise Black ancestor" and the "daughter" as the potential beneficiary of ancestral knowledge.[12] Through gendered discourse she critiques what recent feminist inquiry has recognized as a neglect of the mother's story in favor of the daughter's. In *Tar Baby,* the daughter does not become a speaking subject at the expense of the mother's silence.[13] Instead, Morrison's text gives voice to both. Although the ancestral mothers, configured in the text as "the women in the trees" and evoked

12. See Morrison, "City Limits, Village Values: Concepts of the Neighborhood in Black Fiction," in *Literature and the Urban Experience: Essays on the City and Literature,* ed. Michael C. Jaye and Ann Chalmer Watt (New Brunswick, 1981), 39. For an excellent analysis of how racial and gendered discourses are simultaneous in the texts of black women writers, see Mae Henderson, "Speaking in Tongues: Dialogics, Dialectics, and the Black Woman Writer's Literary Tradition," in *Changing Our Own Words: Essays on Criticism, Theory, and Writing by Black Women,* ed. Cheryl A. Wall (New Brunswick, 1989), 16–37.

13. See Hirsch, *Mother/Daughter Plot,* 1–27.

in other figures such as Thérèse, hear and recognize Jadine, the problem lies with her inability to hear and recognize them.

Tar Baby is essentially the narrative of Jadine's flight from crisis. Uncertain about whether her white boyfriend, Ryk, in Paris wants to marry her for herself or wants to marry just "any black girl" (48), and distraught over the transcendent beauty and insulting gesture of an African woman dressed in yellow, she flees to the Caribbean to the home of her adoptive parents, where she hopes to "sort out things before going ahead" (48–49). Jadine is actually adopted twice—first by her aunt and uncle, who raise her from the time she becomes an orphan at the age of twelve, and second, by Valerian Street, the wealthy white benefactor who pays for her Sorbonne education. Although her European education leads to a degree in art history and a career as a highly acclaimed fashion model, both adoptions take her further from her actual and metaphorical birthplace and contribute to the emotional and spiritual uncertainty that plagues her. While she is in the process of sorting out the direction for her life, Son, a renegade, intrudes himself into the household. Little by little, his presence throws the entire house into a state of disarray that exposes the hostilities, lies, secrets, and untold narratives that had been concealed under the guise of being "like a family" (49). Yet Son is only partially to blame for the chaos that disrupts the false sense of familial calm. Instead, it is the revelation of mothering gone awry—the secret narrative that Valerian's wife, Margaret, had abused their son Michael when he was a small child—that creates the most serious rupture.

In the wake of the chaos that ensues from this revelation, Jadine and Son become lovers and flee from the island. More than lovers, they attempt to become rescuers of each other. In New York City, she attempts to rescue him from a romanticized view of African-American life and culture. In Eloe, Florida, Son's all-black hometown, he attempts to rescue her from ignorance of and disdain for her cultural heritage. Their fundamental cross-purposes preclude the success of their relationship. Jadine flees from this crisis, first by returning to the island and ultimately by returning to Paris. In trying to find her, Son returns to the Caribbean, where the indigenous blacks try to dissuade him from his search. He ultimately yields to the maternal powers of nature and joins the blind horsemen in the tree-covered hills, who, according to the traditional black myth and folklore of the island, had once been runaway slaves.

Like that of Milkman in *Song of Solomon,* Jadine's quest for self begins with a desire to flee from difficult circumstances. Nevertheless, her quest follows the standard mythic path Joseph Campbell traces through the hero's rites of passage: "separation—initiation—return."[14] In mythopoeic terms, the quest involves a passage through rituals that aim to transform the self. In applying these terms to Jadine, we first have to decide where to begin. The very nature of her orphanage makes it difficult to determine whether her home is defined as Philadelphia, her birthplace and the place where cultural roots are, or as Paris or one of the other cities in which she has lived. As Son vehemently reminds her: "Anybody ask you where you from you give them five towns. You're not *from* anywhere" (266). Thus orphanage in the sense of not being from anywhere makes the determination of the beginning phase of the quest—separation—somewhat difficult. The reader is left with the option of identifying Jadine's home as Paris, the place from which she flees when we meet her in the text.

Because Jadine is unaware of the consequences of negating her heritage, she continually desires acceptance into the otherness of white society and defines herself in terms of white social and cultural values. Because she is separated from the sustenance that a

14. Campbell, *Hero with a Thousand Faces,* 30. For an application of Campbell's analysis to *Tar Baby,* see Josie P. Campbell, "To Sing the Song, to Tell the Tale: A Study of Toni Morrison and Simone Schwarz-Bart," *Comparative Literature Studies,* XXII (1985), 394–412. Also see Craig Werner, "The Briar Patch as Modernist Myth: Morrison, Barthes, and Tar Baby as Is," in *Critical Essays on Toni Morrison,* ed. Nellie McKay (Boston, 1988), 150–67.

recognition and acceptance of her heritage could afford her, she aptly fits Alice Walker's definition of an "assimilated woman."[15] Consequently, she is assimilated into the alienated modern cultural milieu.[16] For Jadine, assimilation is a conscious choice reinforced by education and life-style. Yet throughout the novel, the possibility that others do not accept the self she has become makes her feel increasingly alienated. The opinions of others constantly disrupt her image of herself, and it is just such a disruption that compels her to leave Paris for the Caribbean, where she seeks "to get out of her black skin and be only the person inside—not American—not black—just me. . . . She had sought them [her aunt and uncle] out to touch bases, to sort out things before going ahead with . . . anything" (48–49).

It is possible, on the basis of this expressed desire, to interpret Jadine's trip as a quest to discover her "authentic self."[17] Yet her seeking to deny those aspects of her identity that contribute to the sum total of that authentic self shows how impoverished her sense of self is. Because she seems irrevocably separated from her cultural heritage and has no means of negotiating the conflict between that heritage and her adopted one, she is a cultural orphan. The permanence of this condition is suggested in the static nature of her character. Because her sense of self is based on the rejection of blackness inherent in Western values, her consciousness can never be fully transformed. Morrison ultimately leads the reader to question the efficacy of Jadine's quest.

In light of this interpretation, it is apparent that Jadine's quest begins as an escape or flight from the disquieting circumstances of

15. From an interview Mary Helen Washington conducted with Alice Walker; see Washington, "An Approach to the Study of Black Women Writers," in *But Some of Us Are Brave,* ed. Gloria T. Hull *et al.* (Old Westbury, 1982), 213–14.

16. Morrison argues that the modern notion of alienation is not the same for black and white people. Whereas alienation from one's cultural milieu may be heroic in the work of white authors, for black authors it signals a form of loss that is less than heroic. Jadine's alienation from black people is a consequence of the other culture that produced her. See Morrison, "City Limits, Village Values," 39.

17. Bell, "Self-Seekers."

an interracial relationship. Her fear that Ryk proposed to her because he wanted to marry "any black girl" (48) is the impetus for her escape. The possibility that he sees her as the very self she is consciously trying not to be represents the ultimate rejection. It contradicts her own self-definition. Thus she escapes from this possible rejection by seeking refuge in the home of her white patrons, Valerian and Margaret Street. Morrison uses the context of their island home not only to develop Jadine's character but also to develop the various relationships that illuminate the complexity of her character. In Morrison's words, she

> wanted to be in a place where the characters had no access to any of the escape routes that people have in a large city. . . . It seemed easier to isolate them in a kind of Eden within distance of some civilization, but really outside of it. . . . I wanted them to be in an ideal place. . . . When a crisis occurs, people do not have access to . . . things. The crisis becomes a dilemma and forces the characters to do things that otherwise would not be required of them. All the books I have written deal with characters placed deliberately under enormous duress in order to see of what they are made.[18]

In *Tar Baby,* Morrison makes use of Jadine's return to the Streets' Caribbean household to establish the cultural values upon which her sense of identity is based. Through the intrusion of Son into this household, she dramatizes the inherent conflicts that lie beneath the surface of those values.

But even before the main characters are introduced into the novel, Morrison uses nature to establish the consequence of the white presence in this part of the world. The landscape is one in which men, with the help of slaves imported from Haiti, fold "the earth where there had been no fold" and hollow "her where there had been no hollow" (9). Daisy trees "run their roots deeper, clutching the earth like boys found" (9), and clouds look at each

---

18. McKay, "Interview with Toni Morrison," 417.

other and "break apart in confusion" (10). Neither daisy trees nor orchids survive. Instead, houses grow in the hills. The "poor insulted, brokenhearted river," left to sit in "one place like a grandmother," becomes a "swamp the Haitians called Sein de Vieilles" (10). Together, these images of violated nature and disrupted landscape foreshadow the confusion, rootlessness, and loss of nurturance that mar the lives of the characters.

In Morrison's scheme of things, it is by conscious design that Valerian Street's house is high above the swamp and devoured landscape. The house has "door saddles . . . carved lovingly to perfection" (10), "graceful landscaping," and acclaim as "the most handsomely articulated and blessedly unrhetorical house in the Caribbean" (11), which suggests the misplaced priorities of its owner. Described as one who is indifferent to criticism from others, Valerian is more resident of the greenhouse he has added on than of "the oldest and most impressive" (10) house on the island he supposedly controls. His generally eccentric nature is apparent in the care he gives his greenhouse, described as "a nice place to talk to his ghosts in peace while he transplanted, fed, air-layered, rooted, watered, dried and thinned his plants" (14). The elaborate and fond attention Valerian gives his plants again calls attention to his priorities. Against this excessive care of plants is the absence of concern for other areas of his life, areas he has not attended to or has ceased to care about. For example, "when he knew for certain that Michael [his son] would always be a stranger to him, he built the greenhouse as a place of controlled ever-flowing life to greet death in" (53). We learn that all he reads is mail, "having given up books because the language in them changed so much—stained with rivulets of disorder and meaninglessness" (14). A man who has acquired his wealth through the candy business of his family, Valerian has voluntarily exiled himself from Philadelphia and has come to the island to spend his retirement, which he equates with "dying" (26).

Thus the image the reader obtains of Valerian is one of a man who likes order, control, and solitude. He values form over substance, silence over communication, and is content to stay on the island until his death. His wife, Margaret, is a former pageant winner referred to as the "Principal Beauty of Maine" (11). Theirs is a May-to-December marriage not only in age but in social status. Valerian's family owns a genteel business, but Margaret's family status is signified by their living in a trailer at first, then moving to "a seven-room house the Lordi brothers . . . built with their own hands." But she loves the "trailer best for there the separateness she felt had less room to grown in." In contrast to the candy business of Valerian's family is her father and uncles' business as contractors, but this business makes her parents inaccessible: "So when she got married eight months out of high school, she did not have to leave home, she was already gone; she did not have to leave them; they had already left her. And other than money gifts to them and brief telephone calls, she was still gone. It was always like that: she was gone and other people belonged. She was going up or down stairs, other people seemed to be settled somewhere. . . . It was just her luck to fall in love with and marry a man who had a house bigger than her elementary school" (57).

In contrast to Valerian, who never wants to leave the island, Margaret wants desperately to leave it. She refers to it as a "jungle," where there is nothing to do (26). While he feels rooted on the island, the rootlessness of living between the island and Philadelphia frustrates her and prompts her to consider returning with their son Michael, whom she expects to come for Christmas dinner. Although her exile from the mainland seems to be forced upon her by Valerian, the point here is that their condition as exiles is analogous to that of orphans. Both entail fragmentation and the loss of connection.

Magaret's sense of fragmentation and alienation is illustrated in several ways. For example, she tries to dispel "the occasional forgetfulness that plagued her when she forgot the names and uses of things" (55). Because naming is both how we establish authority and how we communicate, Margaret's forgetfulness is another sign of the loss of connection. Her loss of authority is further illustrated by her failure to give orders to her servants, Sydney and Ondine, "the way she was supposed to." The sheer boredom of her life is described tellingly: "There was nothing . . . for her to do but amuse herself in solitude." The only breaks from this life of solitude and boredom are dinner parties in which Valerian's friends visit, the "men talk . . . about music and money and the Marshall Plan," and the "wives talk . . . around the edge of such matters or drop . . . amusing bits into the conversations" (58). This characterization of Margaret shows why Christmas plans and hopes for Michael's homecoming dominate her thoughts. These plans compensate for her feelings of dislocation, and as the reader learns, they also compensate for withheld love. Likewise, Margaret's desire for "an old-fashioned family Christmas" (32) is simply another attempt to compensate for loss, to invent memories rather than reenact cherished ritual. Again, we have an example of values that place form over substance, gestures over feelings.

If Valerian and Margaret represent the form of order, Sydney and Ondine represent a variation of that form. Morrison illustrates how these two have incorporated the values of their white employers into their own values, contrasts black and white attitudes despite this assimilation, and dramatizes the interplay between the two sets of cultural values that have produced Jadine. We learn that they have worked for the Streets for forty years. Their secure position in the household is signified not only by their longevity with the family but by their getting Valerian to pay their niece's college tuition and his Christmas gift to them of stock. When Sydney overreacts to Son's invasion of the house, Ondine reminds him, "We have a future here, as well as a past, and I tell you I can't pick up and move in with some strange new white folks at my age" (101). Yet their means of acquiring this security are significant. When Valerian observes their "smug" (144) reaction to Son, he realizes that his "aphorisms about loyalty and decency" may have been naive. He grows to regard their behavior as "false . . . Uncle Tom-ish" (144). Though Morrison consciously characterizes Ondine and Sydney as Uncle Toms, she attempts to redeem them by contrasting their total adeptness with Valerian and Margaret's ineptitude at running their own house.[19] Thus the kitchen is described as "Ondine's kitchen" (60), and Sydney handles responsibilities that would otherwise go "waiting for a decision nobody was willing to make." (12).

Implied in Valerian's assessment that Sydney and Ondine are Uncle Tomish is the concept of masking. Morrison explains that a "mask sometimes exists when black people talk to white people."[20] It acts as a "veil," in Ellison's words, to repress the white audience's awareness of its own actions and to conceal the humanity of the black people who wear it.[21] For example, although Sydney and Ondine give the appearance of loyalty and devotion, when Margaret gives them instructions, "they smile . . . a private smile she hated" (58). This smile, which encodes a private disrespect beneath the public show of affection, is a mask. But the best example of the mask appears in a description of how it operates and of how Jadine perceives it: "The black people she knew wanted what she wanted—either steadily and carefully like Sydney and Ondine or uproariously and flashily like theater or media types. But whatever their scam, 'making it' was on their minds and they played the game with house cards, each deck issued and dealt by the house. With white people the rules were even simpler. She needed only to be stunning, and to convince them she was not as smart as they were. Say the obvious, ask stupid questions, laugh with abandon, look interested, and light up at any display of their humanity" (126).

Not only do Sydney and Ondine wear masks, but as Jadine's adopted parents, they teach her by example how to do likewise. Morrison thus implies that Jadine's sense of psychic confusion can be partially attributed to the lessons of the mask. Unfortunately,

19. *Ibid.*, 423.
20. Ruas, *Conversations with American Writers*, 218.
21. Ellison, *Shadow and Act*, 64.

the lessons of the mask, as taught by Ondine and Sydney, encode a "betrayal of ancestral functions."[22] They teach her to substitute appearance or form over reality or substance and to reject the self to become what the other expects. By so doing, they privilege the gaze of the other over the voice of the self as speaking subject. Their silent complicity in "playing the game" affords them the semblance of financial security at the expense of their integrity. They become trickster figures, masking their true desires. Yet as the recent scholarship of Henry Louis Gates reminds us, the trickster figure in African-American folklore encodes a "multiplicity of meanings."[23] At the same time that Sydney and Ondine mask their own desires, they also mask their ability to read (interpret) the Streets to their advantage. By parodying themselves into carnivalesque figures, they assume what Mikhail Bakhtin identifies as folkloric strategies for interrogating power relations between cultures in a given community.[24] Thus the masks enable Morrison to critique the "familial" arrangements at work in the Street household. By extension, she calls into question the values that are reproduced in Jadine and that deny her the cultural rootedness she seeks. In denying identity, the mask denies connecting rootedness.

On the island, then, reside the adults who have produced Jadine. Like Valerian and Margaret, Sydney and Ondine are exiles. But in that they have separated themselves from other black

22. Morrison, "City Limits, Village Values," 42.

23. Henry Louis Gates, Jr., *The Signifying Monkey: A Theory of Afro-American Literary Criticism* (New York, 1988), 19. As Dale Bauer argues, the silence that accompanies the mask does not challenge cultural domination but helps to perpetuate it. In African-American folklore, however, the mask, a sign of the trickster, is considered a subversive strategy that enables survival at the same time that it critiques structures of domination. Both notions are related to Bakhtin's notion of parody and carnival. See Bauer, *Feminist Dialogics: A Theory of Failed Community* (Albany, 1988), 1–15.

24. Mikhail Bakhtin, "Forms of Time and Chronotope in the Novel," in *The Dialogic Imagination: Four Essays by M. M. Bakhtin,* ed. Michael Holquist, trans. Caryl Emerson and Michael Holquist (Austin, 1981), 158–63.

people, they are doubly exiled just as Jadine is doubly adopted—first by them and then by her white benefactors.[25] Morrison suggests the dubious nurturing that Jadine has received, therefore, through her characterization of the people Jadine identifies as family. In Jadine's fluctuating between claiming that her aunt and uncle "were family" and feeling they could live together "like family" (49), Morrison reinforces her adopted status with them. In her claim that Valerian and Margaret "educated" (118) her and that she is "family now—or nobody" (68), she reinforces the literal and symbolic irony of her adopted status. What becomes interesting about this household is Jadine's place in it. Rather than downstairs near her blood relatives in their servants' quarters, she sleeps upstairs adjacent to Margaret, an arrangement that further emphasizes the origin of her values, her distance from other black people, including her relatives, and her inherent motherlessness, despite those who claim her as a daughter. The sleeping arrangement reinforces that she is caught between the world of black assimilation and the world of wasted time, money, and values in a liminal space of rootlessness.

Ironically, it is Michael, Valerian and Margaret's conspicuously absent son, who first tries to caution Jadine about the error of her ways. Although Michael does not appear for most of the novel, the reader is aware of his importance because Christmas plans revolve around his mother's frenzied anticipation of his arrival, even though he customarily avoids coming home for any reason. His absence is made even more conspicuous when the revelation that Margaret abused him as a child disrupts the Christmas dinner far more than his failure to arrive. Unlike his parents, who seem to admire Jadine's success in the white world with a mixture of benign indifference and awe, Michael questions "why [she] was studying art history at the snotty school instead of . . . orga-

25. Campbell, "To Sing the Song," 396. For an interesting discussion of how their positionality is related to class issues in Morrison, see Barbara Christian, *Black Feminist Criticism: Perspectives on Black Women Writers* (New York, 1985), 71–80.

nizing or something." He admonishes her for "abandoning [her] history . . . [her] people" (72). It is especially ironic that he cautions her not to be the very thing Valerian accuses him of being: "a purveyor of exotics, a typical anthropologist, a cultural orphan who sought other cultures he could love without risk or pain" (145).

We cannot assume that Valerian's judgment of Michael is valid, for he is still harboring disappointment that Michael did not want to take over the candy business. Ironically, Valerian went into the family business "out of respect for the industry" (52). He is, therefore, in the tradition, if not the spirit, of capitalism and has no respect for Michael's socialist political leanings, his anthropological pursuits, or his insistent desire "for value in life, not money" (199). His apparent estrangement from both parents makes Michael an orphan in the spiritual sense of the word. But the concern here is not with Michael per se but with his valid assessment of Jadine. That he "wanted value in his life, not money," and that he spends his life encouraging people to "keep their own heritage intact" (199), suggest that he is a kind of foil for Jadine. That is, he underscores her flawed sense of self, her rootlessness, and her loss of concern for and connection to her own people.

The validity of Michael's judgment of Jadine is apparent in her response to it: "I knew what I was leaving. It wasn't like he thought: all grits and natural grace. But he did make me want to apologize for what I was doing, what I felt. For liking 'Ave Maria' better than gospel music. . . . Picasso *is* better than an Itumba mask. The fact that he was intrigued by them is proof of his genius, not the mask-makers'" (74). Morrison achieves a great deal in this exchange of ideas. She invokes her folk aesthetic by revealing Jadine's negative, stereotypical opinions of ethnic food and African-American music. Having been raised by her aunt and uncle to mirror rather than question white Western values, she rejects what those values reject. Jadine's reaction to the explicit indictment in Michael's questions is a sign of her rejection of her heritage as well as a sign that no one has taught her to value that heritage or the cultural narratives that would make her affirm it. That she values Picasso's work over the African masks that inspired it only reiterates the distortion of her values. Ironically, although she describes Michael as "clearheaded—independent" (72), she gives no credence to his cautionary words. Jadine's attitude toward her own culture recalls black historian Carter G. Woodson's dictum: "The education of any people should begin with the people themselves, but Negroes . . . have been dreaming about the ancients of Europe and about those who have tried to imitate them."[26] It is also ironic that Jadine refers to art to justify imitation, for it calls attention to her own miseducation, or at least to her inability to be an artist: "She loved to paint and draw so it was unfair not to be good at it. Still she . . . [felt] lucky to know it, to know the difference between fine and mediocre, so she'd put that instinct to work and studied art history—there she was never wrong" (182).

In portraying Jadine as an unsuccessful artist, Morrison recalls the image of two other thwarted artist figures—Pauline Breedlove in *The Bluest Eye,* who "missed—without knowing what she missed—paints and crayons"—and Sula Peace in *Sula,* who "like any artist with no art form . . . became dangerous."[27] More than her privileged status and access to an art form, it is her contentment with being an observer of art rather than being an artist that distances Jadine from these two black female characters in Morrison's first two novels. Moreover, Jadine's enchantment with European art distances her from the indigenous art of African culture. Morrison draws an image of Jadine as one who chooses the path of least resistance—to study rather than to do—a path that requires no risk or responsibility. Thus it is she, not Michael, who is truly the cultural orphan.

26. Carter G. Woodson, *The Miseducation of the Negro* (Washington, D.C., 1903), 33.

27. See Toni Morrison, *The Bluest Eye* (New York, 1970), 89, and Morrison, *Sula* (New York, 1973), 105.

In describing the unique position of the artist in the African-American community, historian Lerone Bennett asserts that "an artist in a segregated society which questions the humanity of all Negroes, whether they peel potatoes or write poems, has special responsibilities and special tasks . . . to break through to authenticity . . . to come to terms with [oneself] and [one's] history, to accept [oneself], to accept the color of [one's] skin and accept the ambiguity and tension of one's experience."[28] By his very absence, Michael calls attention to the inauthenticity that characterizes his father's house. His repeated failure to show up not only calls into question his relationship with his mother but also suggests his refusal to accept his parents' vacuous values. His excursions into other cultures and his advocacy of a return to a simpler economic system reflect not just on his father's life-style but on Western patriarchal values in general. In explaining why *Tar Baby* opens with a retired candy executive rather than Jadine, Morrison explains that he is the center of the household because white men run the world and "that's pretty much the way it is."[29] Thus Michael serves as a forerunner to Son, the renegade intruder whose presence threatens to topple the tenuous calm that holds the house of exiles intact. His arrival not only precipitates a disruption in the household, but it offers Jadine her first chance to "break through to authenticity" and to embrace her own cultural heritage. He is thus the guide for her spiritual quest for self.

One important image in *Tar Baby* is the mirror. Like the mask, Morrison uses it to signify the theme of identity and authenticity. In the middle of her conversation with Valerian about Michael, Jadine notices that Valerian's eyes are "without melanin, they were all reflection, like mirrors, chamber after chamber, corridor after corridor of mirrors, each one taking its shape from the other and giving it back as its own until final effect was color where no color existed at all" (74). Although the significance of what Jadine

28. Quoted in Jeanne Noble, *Beautiful Also Are the Souls of My Black Sisters* (Englewood Cliffs, N.J., 1978), 111.
29. Ruas, *Conversations with American Writers,* 225.

sees eludes her, it is not lost to the reader. Valerian's eyes reflect what he has created. As the head of the household, he has not only created Jadine but, in a sense, recreated the people around him—Margaret, Sydney, and Ondine—so that the entire household reflects his values. But as the description of his eyes suggests, these values are meaningless; they deny color, and, by implication, they deny the difference or identity of others. For Valerian, appearances are acceptable substitutes for reality because he cannot see outside of himself to recognize the identity of another. As Jessica Benjamin asserts: "The paradox of recognition, the need for acknowledgment that turns us back to dependence on the other, brings about a struggle for control. This struggle can result in the realization that if we fully negate the other, that is, if we assume complete control over him and destroy his identity and will, then we have negated ourselves as well."[30] Jadine enjoys the illusion of being no color at all at the same time that she unknowingly suffers from the negation of her identity.

The image of the mirror recalls W. E. B. Du Bois' prophetic description of the peculiar situation of being black in a country that at once denies and scorns the identity of black people: "The Negro is . . . born with a veil, and gifted with second-sight in this American world,—a world which yields him no true self-consciousness, but only lets him see himself through the revelation of the other world. It is a peculiar sensation, this double-consciousness, this sense of always looking at one's self through the eyes of others, of measuring one's soul by the tape of a world that looks on in amused contempt and pity. One ever feels his twoness—an American, a Negro; two souls, two thoughts, two unreconciled strivings."[31] Morrison's portrayal of Jadine as a cultural orphan suggests the futility of her attempts to measure herself against Valerian. Moreover, her problem is more complex because she does not acknowledge that she is black. Thus her quest

30. Benjamin, *Bonds of Love*, 39.

31. W. E. B. Du Bois, *The Souls of Black Folk* (1903; rpr. New York, 1968), 15–16.

involves a series of challenges to her inauthentic existence, to her denial of her essential self.

The most significant of these challenges, of course, is represented by Son, and in her initial reaction to him we see the extent to which she has adopted the same values as the Streets. Her first reaction is so similar to Margaret's that Son asks her, "Why you little white girls always think somebody's trying to rape you?" Her response is, "White? I'm not . . . you know I'm not white!" Though it may appear insignificant that she halts in midsentence and changes "I'm not" to "you know," Morrison uses this shift to signify Jadine's inability to admit she is not white at the same time that she wants Son to be precise about her color. Her caution for him not to pull "that black woman white woman shit on [her]" reveals two emotions: on one hand, she wants to stress her superiority over him; on the other, she resents the threat he poses for her sense of self. When she vents her self-hatred, it appears in the form of name-calling—"ape," "nigger," "baboon," and "animal"—names that suggest that she is more emotionally overwrought about his presence than Margaret is (121).

Son's invasion of the household has implications for each member. Because Margaret finds him hiding in her closet, "in [her] things" (79), she is initially the most alarmed. He evokes not only her deepest racial fears but an intense panic that her Christmas plans are ruined. For Sydney and Ondine he is a threat to the material security they have worked for and the colorless life they have tried to lead. For Jadine, not only is he a threat to her belongings and physical body, but she sees him as a threat to her illusion of being colorless as well. For Valerian, Son is the "forepresence of Michael" (143), someone he can rescue from "Margaret's hysteria" (144) as he used to rescue Michael, who, as a child, used to sing in loneliness "under the sink" (76). Thus Valerian's decision to let Son stay is an act of rebellion. It is an expression of the "disappointment nudging contempt for the outrage Jade and Sydney and Ondine exhibited in defending property and personnel that did not belong to them from a black man who was one of their own. As the evening progressed, Valerian thoroughly enjoyed the disarray that his invitation had thrown them into" (145). Son's arrival disrupts the apparent calm and exposes the hidden underlying tensions. As Susan Willis describes it, he brings an "eruption of funk."[32] Put another way, in Son's disruption of the household with the very reminders of blackness and African-American culture that Jadine has tried to avoid, he is a sign of the folk aesthetic in *Tar Baby*. As the relationship between them develops, Jadine's character as a cultural orphan is more fully delineated.

Their first meeting, once he is discovered in the house, takes place as she steps out of the shower to find him standing in front of her mirror. The mirror figures strongly in this scene as an image of identity. Jadine struggles "to pull herself away from his image in the mirror" (114) and thus symbolically seeks to deny that there is any shared identity to acknowledge. Her staring at his "wild, aggressive, vicious . . . uncivilized, reform school . . . Mau Mau, Attica, chain-gang hair" (113) stresses that she is able to see his image only in the most negative terms. She does not view her own image as long as he is in her room. Once he leaves, however, she feels an intense desire to "clean him off her" (122), for "he had jangled something in her that was so repulsive, so awful, and he managed to make her feel that the thing that repelled her was not in him but in her" (123).

But the resentment and hostility Jadine feels for Son give way to time and circumstances. After two weeks, a shave, and some of Valerian's clothes, he seems "beautiful" (130) enough that she is "more frightened of his good looks than she had been by his ugliness" (158). She consents to his request to go to the beach with him but remains "buried behind the screen, the wall of her sketch pad" (170). When they try to engage in conversation, the differences between them become even more obvious than before. The differences can be almost wholly summed up in the fact that

32. Willis, "Eruptions of Funk," 269.

he is from Eloe, an "all black" (172) town in Florida, whereas she is from "Baltimore. Philadelphia. Paris" (173). In saying that she is from three places, she confirms his indictment that she is "not *from* anywhere" (266). While he has roots and values "fraternity," she is rootless and values only herself. Yet in the sense that he is an anarchic wanderer who is "propertyless, homeless" (168), he is reminiscent of Michael. Like Michael, he has chosen to live outside of traditional standards and mores. Yet the lure of Jadine, the tar baby Valerian has created, draws Son into the Street household, and he becomes an exile along with the others. What is significant about the trip to the beach is that it foreshadows the role he will play as a guide into her cultural heritage.

But the scene at the beach is more important for what it reveals about Jadine than for what we learn about Son. Jadine's slip into the black jungle muck near the beach is one of the most symbolic episodes in the novel, for in that scene she literally becomes a tar baby. Although the full complexity of the term is clear only at the end of the novel, part of its significance becomes apparent. Jadine's fall establishes her as the tar baby physically, because of the color of the substance, and metaphorically, because of its ability to entrap. That the substance sticks to Jadine signifies the blackness of her skin that she has continued to reject despite the futility of doing so. Moreover, the substance, through its adhesive quality, symbolizes the inevitable attraction between Son and Jadine. In commenting on her use of the tar baby folktale, Morrison says: "I found that there is a tar baby in African mythology. I started thinking about tar. At one time, a tar pit was a holy place, at least an important place, because tar was used to build things. It came naturally out of the earth; it held things together. . . . For me, the tar baby came to mean the black woman who can hold things together."[33] Hence Morrison draws on the positive connotations of the folk myth to deepen her portrait of Jadine. The scene at the muck symbolizes how the folk aesthetic operates in this novel. It

33. Le Clair, "Language Must Not Sweat," 27.

serves to produce countermyth to the mythic quest of one who assumes she can ignore her true identity.[34]

As Jadine realizes she is slipping, she thinks, "There is an easy way to get out of this . . . and every Girl Scout knows what it is but I don't" (182). Just as she feels she is in "strange waters" (126) with a black man like Son, in the muck she is literally in territory for which her inauthentic life has not prepared her. Moreover, the reference to Girl Scouts suggests she has not had the benefit of hearing those female narratives that could teach her how to adapt to new circumstances. Furthermore, in her rejection of the women in the trees, who are also part of the scene at the muck, she rejects the stories they could teach her about how to be an authentic black woman.

The scene at the muck also has sexual overtones. In an attempt to keep from sinking further, she tightens her arms around a tree that sways "as though it wished to dance with her" (182). Her thoughts convey the sexual connotations of her actions: "Don't sweat or you'll lose your partner, the tree. Cleave together like lovers. Press together like man and wife. Cling to your partner, hang on to him and never let him go. Creep upon him a millimeter at a time, slower than the slime and cover him like the moss. Caress his bark and finger his ridges. Sway when he sways and shiver with him too. Whisper your numbers from one to fifty into the parts that have been lifted away and left tender skin behind. Love him and trust him with your life because you are up to your kneecaps in rot" (182–83).

Nothing in the text up to this point prepares the reader for thoughts like these from Jadine. In fact, they do not seem to be her thoughts at all, but possibly those of the women in the trees. There are at least two possible interpretations of this soliloquy. One is its contrast with the earlier scene in which her assumption that Son wants to rape her evokes thoughts of copulating dogs:

34. In using the term *countermyth*, I borrow from Hortense Spillers' description and Craig Werner's analysis. See Spillers, "Cross-Currents, Discontinuities: Black Women's Fiction," in *Conjuring: Black Women, Fiction, and Literary Tradition*, ed. Marjorie Pryse and Hortense Spillers (Bloomington, 1985), 251.

"One dog sniffing at the hindquarters of another, and the female, her back to him, not moving, but letting herself be sniffed . . . the bitch never minding that the male never looked in her face . . . or that he had just come up out of nowhere, smelled her ass and stuck his penis in. . . . She had done nothing but be 'in heat' . . . I felt sorry for her. . . . [I] decided then and there at the age of twelve in Baltimore never to be broken in the hands of any man" (123–24). Thus the scene at the muck could represent her revised, transformed attitude toward her own sexuality in general and toward Son in particular. The other possible interpretation of her thoughts is that they are an extension of those of the omniscient narrator. That is, if we interpret *Tar Baby* as a cautionary tale, which it seems to be, then these words are actually Morrison's direct address to her female hero and hence to other black women. Yet the last phrase, "you are up to your kneecaps in rot" (183), seems to undercut both interpretations in the language we *do* associate with Jadine. It suggests that her actions have been those of survival and nothing more. In that Son and Jadine become romantically involved, the scence is ultimately a foreshadowing of their relationship as lovers.

It is probably their mutual involvement in breaking up the Christmas dinner dispute, as well as their status as "guests," that finally brings them together. The fight exposes all the tensions of class, race, and hatred that had been repressed, seething beneath the cover of silence and normalcy. The real substance of the lives disrupts the form, truth disrupts the silence, and what had been private becomes public. In this scene all the repressed narratives of the household break through the facade of peaceful coexistence; the stories that mothers and/or mother figures have or have not told become central rather than hidden. Although the dispute begins when Ondine is offended that *her* two servants were fired, it ends with Ondine's revelation that Margaret abused Michael as a child. As Peter Erickson argues, this is one of the most crucial scenes in the novel.[35] Not only does it call into ques-

35. Erickson, "Images of Nurturance," 12–13.

tion Margaret's preoccupation with whether Michael would come home for Christmas, which he does not, but it raises the issue of mothering. Nearly every character in the novel is discussed either directly or indirectly in terms of mothering. Even a minor character, Gideon, one of the two servants fired, is called "Yardman, as though he had not been mothered" (161). From Jadine, the literal orphan, to Margaret, who felt like an orphan, to Ondine, who tries to mother Michael first and then Jadine, mothers have been an issue. When Jadine and Son fall in love, flee the island, and begin living together in New York, for the first time she "gradually . . . came to feel unorphaned" (229).

The dynamics of their relationship change in New York. While he makes her feel unorphaned and gives "her a brand-new childhood" (229), she gives "him the balance he was losing, the ballast and counterweight to the stone of sorrow New York City had given him" (217). They tell "each other everything" (225), but what is interesting is that he shares folktales—his African-American cultural heritage—while she shares identities or choices she once thought were her only options until she went to Europe: to "marry a dope king or a doctor, model, or teach art" (225). By telling her the stories of "The Fox and Stork, The Monkey and The Lion, The Spider Goes to the Market" (225), he attempts to reorient her to the heritage she denies. Again the folk aesthetic is injected into the narrative as countermyth to the heritage she has adopted. But there are signs that her heritage still eludes her in that she thinks of their sex life in terms of "adventure and fantasy" (225), and she speaks of her aunt and uncle in fairy-tale language when she says, "We'll get rich and send for them and live happily ever after" (226).

In a sense, the life they lead in New York *is* a fairy tale. They play out husband and wife roles of "nestling" (226). She thinks of making genuine paella and finishing macrame plant holders, and he fixes the dishwasher. And in the tradition of a fairy tale he sees "it all as a rescue: first tearing her mind away from the blinding awe. Then the physical escape from the plantation" (219). He feels he has been looking for her all his life, and "if he loved and lost this woman . . . he would surely lose the world" (220). She views the change as a rescue in a sense as well: "This is home, she thought with an orphan's delight; not Paris, not Baltimore, not Philadelphia. This is home. . . . And now she would take it; take it and give it to Son. They would make it theirs. She would show it, reveal it to him, live it with him" (222).

Yet, just as they tell two different kinds of narratives, they have two different ideas of home. Despite her efforts, "he insisted on Eloe" (223), so they leave for his hometown. As the last phase of her quest, Eloe is where Son ultimately hopes to reorient Jadine to her cultural roots. Of course, he is unsuccessful. She resents "being shunted off with Ellen and the children while the men grouped on the porch and, after a greeting, ignored her" (246). The small, windowless room she has to sleep in makes her feel "she might as well have been in a cave, a grave, the dark womb of the earth, suffocating with the sound of plant life moving, but deprived of its sight" (252). She ultimately finds Eloe "rotten and more boring than ever. A burnt-out place [with] . . . no life" (259). The language Morrison uses to describe Eloe not only inscribes Jadine's critique of it but calls attention to her inability to accept its regenerative capabilities. Morrison's description recalls James Hillman's analysis of how such scenes function in narrative fiction: "The land of the dead is the country of ancestors, and the images who walk in on us are our ancestors. If not literally, the blood and genes from whom we descend, then they are the historical progenitors, or archetypes, of our particular spirit informing it with ancestral culture."[36] Jadine's inability to recognize or connect with the women of Eloe signifies this rejection of ancestral maternity and culture. She returns to New York without Son and feels "orphaned again" (260).

The inability of each to live in the home of the other results in a confrontation once they are together again in New York. Each

---

36. James Hillman, *Healing Fiction* (New York, 1983), 60.

attempts to confront the other with the truth. She says the truth is that while he engaged in activities like hiding from sheriffs and lawyers, she was "learning how to make it in *this* world" (264). Son responds: "The truth is that whatever you learned in those colleges that didn't include me ain't shit. . . . If they didn't teach you that, they didn't teach you nothing, because until you know about me, you don't know nothing about yourself" (264). At the height of their confrontation, he attempts to tell her the "tar baby" (270) tale, but it is too late. In other words, Son tries to counter the fairy tales that have shaped her life with the African-American folk narrative he feels she has failed to listen to or learn from. But her cultural heritage, as he knows it, has no meaning for her. Indeed, Jadine's inability to appreciate the meaning of this cultural narrative—that is, the tar baby folktale—is a sign that the absence of such narratives precludes her consciousness from being transformed. She and Son attempt to sustain a relationship for a short time thereafter, but the reality of the cross-purposes that underlie their relationship surfaces again: "This rescue was not going well. She thought she was rescuing him from the night women who wanted him for themselves, wanted him feeling superior in a cradle, deferring to him; wanted to settle for wifely competence when she could be almighty, to settle for fertility rather than originality, nurturing instead of building. He thought he was rescuing her from Valerian, meaning *them,* the aliens, the people who in a mere three hundred years had killed a world millions of years old" (269). The question in her mind is, "Mama-spoiled black man, will you mature with me?" His question for her is, "Culture-bearing black woman, whose culture are you bearing?" (269). He almost changes for her, but as his question indicates, it is dangerous to change for someone whose own sense of self is borrowed, not intact. Thus they arrive at a cul-de-sac.

This final conflict results in her feeling like a "closed away orphan" (271), and he ends up looking at photos of his family and friends in Eloe that Jadine took and thinking as she did that they looked "stupid, backwoodsy and dumb" (273). That her influence

makes him question his cultural roots and sense of identity suggests the negative connotations of the tar baby tale. He appears
stuck in a life-denying trap. She, by contrast, has her illusion of
freedom intact. She assumes that the key to success is to "forget
the past and do better" (271). Thus she goes full circle. She escapes
a confrontation with her sense of self by fleeing once again. Her
quest ends with her return to Paris. Unlike the triumphant conclusion to Milkman's quest in *Song of Solomon*, Jadine's ends in a
questionable triumph. She is alone by herself in a restaurant feeling "proud of having been so decisive, so expert at the leaving.
Of having refused to be broken in the big ugly hands of any
man." In that she feels "lean and male" and that her "aloneness
tasted good" (275), Jadine distances herself from all the women
in the novel—mythic and real. Thus when she leaves for Paris at
the end of the novel, she is escaping more than Son. She is escaping her cultural heritage, her sense of "femaleness," her sense
of self.

Jadine's attempt to escape her female self emerges as the most
significant dimension of the novel. From the woman in yellow,
to the women in the trees, to the night women at Eloe, all the
women in the novel question some aspect of Jadine's womanhood.
The woman in yellow is the presence of the African past undefiled
by Western standards. She continues to haunt Jadine long after
the insulting gesture in Paris because she represents a "woman's
woman . . . mother/sister/she; that unphotographable beauty"
(46). Her authentic beauty and fertility, symbolized in the three
eggs she carries, contrast with Jadine's fashion-model beauty and
disdain for fertility. The women in the trees represent the African-
American slavery past. They combine myth and folk legend in
that they are the "swamp women [who] mate with horsemen in
the hills" (184), according to the mythic legend told on the island.
Because the horsemen in the myth are blind runaway slaves, they
are history as well as legend. The women in the trees first see
Jadine as a restored "runaway child" when she falls into the muck.
But they quickly realize in their "arrogant . . . femaleness" that

she has forgotten her "sacred properties" and is trying to get away from them (183). Finally, the night women at Eloe represent all women in general but the women of her familial past in particular. When Jadine and Son are in Eloe, all the women of her life converge into the night women who come into the room when she and Son begin to make love: "Cheyenne [Son's dead wife] got in, and then the rest: Rosa and Thérèse and Son's dead mother . . . Ondine and Soldier's wife Ellen and . . . her own dead mother and even the woman in yellow. All there crowding into the room. Some of them she did not know, recognize, but they were all there spoiling her love-making, taking away her sex like succubi, but not his. . . . They each pulled out a breast and showed it to her. . . . 'I have breasts too,' she said or thought or willed. . . . But they didn't believe her" (258). Clearly all these women symbolize Jadine's refusal to define herself on the basis of cultural heritage, historical tradition, and familial past. In denying these women, however, she denies her own mother. As Adrienne Rich describes this denial, it is "matrophobia—rebellion against the imposed female image," a denial that results in a tragic "splitting of the self."[37] That the images of women haunt her suggests that psychic wholeness will elude her until she comes to terms with her black and female self.

Before Jadine returns to Paris, she goes to the island to gather her belongings. Ondine wonders whether she would have bothered to say good-bye if she had not forgotten her sealskin coat. Nevertheless, she decides to tell Jadine what it means to be a woman: "I never told you nothing at all and I take full responsibility for that. But I have to tell you something now. . . . Jadine, a girl has got to be a daughter first. She have to learn that. And

---

37. Adrienne Rich, *Of Woman Born: Motherhood as Experience and Institution* (New York, 1986), 235–37. Also see Davis, "Self, Society, and Myth." Davis questions whether and how Morrison would conceive of the female mode of heroism, but she does not include Tar Baby in her analysis. Although I do not consider Morrison's discourse of motherhood to be problematic, some feminists might. For an analysis of a way out of this debate, see Hirsch, *Mother/Daughter Plot,* 8–16.

if she never learns how to be a daughter, she can't never learn how to be a woman: a woman good enough for a child; good enough for a man—good enough even for the respect of other women . . . you don't need your own natural mother to be a daughter" (281). Jadine mistakenly assumes that her aunt wants her to "parent," and she corrects her by saying she simply wants her to know that "a daughter is a woman who cares about where she come from and takes care of them that took care of her" (281). Ondine's words encode the revisionist perspective of familial discourse that is at work throughout the novel. Unfortunately, the message Ondine shares comes too late to be of any avail. Jadine argues that "there are other ways to be a woman. . . . Your way is one . . . but it's not my way. I don't want to be . . . like you" (282). No resolution comes of their discussion. As in her relationship with Son, she and Ondine arrive at a narrative cul-de-sac. Jadine feels her motherlessness more acutely, and Ondine feels she has failed twice as a mother—first in "telling nobody" about Margaret's maternal crime of child abuse, and second in not telling Jadine, "another one not from [her] womb" (283), sooner what she needed to know about being a daughter. Thus in the tradition of the folktale after which it is named, *Tar Baby* warns that the absence of cultural narrative destroys not only the self but the single most important connection between the self and others. Moreover, Ondine's silence is a sign that Jadine not only has not heard the narratives that would teach her how to be a daughter but that she also has not heard the stories that would teach her how to be a woman in the tradition of her African-American heritage. Morrison suggests that by her silence Ondine has been remiss as both a woman and a mother. We recall that Ondine at one point regards her mothering of Jadine as ideal in that "it was without the stress of a mother-daughter relationship" (96). As the end of the novel reveals, the stress beneath the veneer of being "like a family" was there the whole time. It merely needed a catalyst to appear.

As her guide, Son had been that catalyst. But unlike the traditional questing myth, the guide, not the hero, is triumphant at the end. Thérèse warns Son to "forget her [Jadine]. . . . She has forgotten her ancient properties" (305). When she leads him onto the island of blind horsemen, the message is clear. He has escaped the tar baby and is free to return to nature or the "earth mother" to live with the mythical reality of blindness rather than the historical reality of clear vision. Unlike their rejection of Jadine, the mythic women in the trees step "back . . . to make the way easier for a certain kind of man" (306).

Toni Morrison's own moral vision emerges from this complex portrayal of Jadine. She says her novels "should clarify roles that have become obscured; they ought to identify those things in the past that are useful and those things that are not; and they ought to give nourishment."[38] The reader is left to question whether the roles really have been clarified. As one critic argues, in the role of daughter Morrison is sympathetic with Jadine's plight, but in the role of mother she is skeptical and critical.[39] The daughter appears in Jadine's lament that "every orphan knew that . . . mothers however beautiful were not fair" (288), while the mother appears with the reminder of "ancient properties" (305). This mother-daughter conflict possibly reflects Morrison's own divided consciousness. In one interview she explains that the consequence of "not paying attention to the ancient properties—which . . . means the ability to be the 'ship' *and* the 'safe harbor,'" Jadine loses "the tar quality, the ability to hold something together that otherwise would fall apart—which is what [she] mean[t] by . . . nurturing."[40]

Yet when we recall Morrison's comments about the "Ulysses theme, the leaving home . . . that has always been the most attractive feature about black male life," we see her representing the mythic quest in her novels primarily in a mimetic sense.[41] That is,

38. LeClair, "Language Must Not Sweat," 26.
39. Erickson, "Images of Nurturance," 29.
40. Wilson, "Conversation with Toni Morrison," 133.
41. Stepto, "Intimate Things in Place," in *Chant of Saints,* ed. Harper and Stepto, 226–27.

the quest, in male terms, has positive implications for her male heroes and negative ones for her female heroes. When we think of Sula, Pilate, and Jadine, we question whether Morrison resolves her dilemma of how to portray the female hero's quest. Jadine appears triumphant in her freedom only to a point. She achieves the hero's sense of awareness only in realizing "there were no shelters anyway" (288) and that "perhaps . . . the thing Ondine was saying [was] . . . a grown woman did not need safety or its dreams" (290). Yet we are not convinced that Jadine will ever be able to combine the nest and the adventure, the journey out with the return home. Instead, the absence of narrative has meant a quest with no epiphany, a journey without the benefit of a trans-formed consciousness.

Morrison's folk aesthetic and mythic impulse take a different turn in this novel. The folk aesthetic is marginalized in one sense to suggest how the contemporary black woman who denies her history and culture marginalizes her authentic self. She achieves this effect by adapting the famous folktale to myth to affirm free-dom to venture outside of male restrictions in the tradition of the quest. In explaining her adaptation of the tar baby folk myth, Morrison says she saw it as "history and prophecy."[42] She means for the reader to question the freedom of the "contemporary woman" who neglects the "essentials from the past."[43] *Tar Baby,* then, is a cautionary folktale for our times. Toni Morrison affirms the heroic quest of women, but she also affirms the value of the return to the nest, the place of nurturance. She assures us that we will know ourselves only inasmuch as we recognize our own stories in the stories of both our mothers and our sisters.

42. Le Clair, "Language Must Not Sweat," 27.
43. Ruas, *Conversations with American Writers,* 229.

CONCLUSION

TELLING STORIES FOR A CHANGE: WOMEN WRITERS AND THE CULTURAL FUNCTION OF NARRATIVE

> So many of these new folk nowadays . . . seem to have neither past nor future. Conversation's got to have some root in the past.
> —Sarah Orne Jewett, *Country of the Pointed Firs*

> For people who have been culturally parochial for a long time, the novel is the transition. The novel has to provide the richness of the past as well as suggestions of what the use of it is.
> —Toni Morrison

> There are two lasting gifts we can give our children—one is roots, the other is wings.
> —Anonymous

All narratives move in at least two directions at once—toward recovering the past and toward being heard or told. They grow out of the roots of history, memory, and culture, and they take flight on the wings of desire. This perpetual interplay between history and memory, remembering and telling, prompted Walter Benjamin to claim that "storytelling is always the art of repeating stories."[1] But as this study has argued, there are differences between the stories women tell and the ones men tell, just as there are differences in our ways of knowing and ordering experience.[2] While men's stories tend to be linear, circularity dominates women's stories and blurs boundaries between male-constructed op-

1. Walter Benjamin, "The Storyteller," in *Illuminations,* ed. Hannah Arendt (New York, 1969), 91.
2. See Mary Field Belenky, Blythe McVicker Clinchy, Nancy Rule Goldberger, and Jill Mattuck Tarule, eds., *Women's Ways of Knowing* (New York, 1986), 100–52.

positions of past and present, old and young, city and country, self and other. Moreover, there are differences between what men value as the stuff of fiction and what women value. In her essay "City Limits, Village Values: Concepts of the Neighborhood in Black Fiction," Toni Morrison argues that "the assumptions of white writers are markedly different from those of Black ones." Whereas the "anti-urbanism" of white writers reveals "private codes of self-discipline, endurance and stubborn individualism," the black writer's "literary view of the city and his concept of its opposite, the village or country, is more telling than the predictable and rather obvious responses of mainstream American writers to post-industrial decay, dehumanization and the curtailing of individualism which they imagined existed in the city but not in the country." [3] As I have attempted to prove, however, the boundaries of race manifest themselves differently in women and men. Consequently, this cross-cultural study is based on the discovery that Sarah Orne Jewett and Toni Morrison wrote as culture workers—cultural archivists and redemptive scribes to affirm "village values." Whereas men's literature validates the individual quest or journey out more than the return home, women's literature validates both the individual journey out and the return to home and community.

Yet because narratives are culture-specific, different myths and folklore inform the fiction of these two writers. Each writer sought not just to reclaim cultural resources and "discredited knowledge" but to critique those forms of cultural domination that would devalue and marginalize those resources. Their fiction necessarily reflects their very different eras, cultural backgrounds, racial identities, and places of origin. Whereas the mother-daughter plot of Demeter and Persephone seems to inform Jewett's sketches and novels, African-American configurations of "three household women" inform Morrison's fiction. [4] Jewett's fiction privileges mother figures and goddesses, but the

---

3. Morrison, "City Limits, Village Values," 36–37.
4. Willis, *Specifying*, 165.

historical reality of slavery and its consequences require Morrison to inscribe not just the issue of mothering in her fiction but also the condition of motherlessness and the importance of ancestors. Nowhere are these distinctions more apparent than in the way these two writers conflate the concerns of death and motherhood. Thus a brief examination of Jewett's "ghost" story "The Foreigner" (1900) and Morrison's most recent novel, *Beloved* (1987), a ghost story of sorts, illustrates some of the interesting dynamics of gender and narrative in the fiction of these two women writers. More important, these two texts reiterate some of the basic assumptions this cross-cultural study has attempted to explore and lead to some of the conclusions we can draw.

In "The Foreigner" the reader is allowed once again to bear witness to, "to overhear," a conversation between Mrs. Todd and the narrator.[5] The storminess of the night causes Mrs. Todd to become uncharacteristically anxious about her mother, Mrs. Blackett, and to worry about how her other village neighbors are coping. As the narrator observes Mrs. Todd, she reflects, "The families of sailors and coastwise adventures by sea must always be worrying about somebody, this side of the world or the other" (159). Not only does the narrator's thought foreshadow an actual event in the story, but it inscribes the textual strategy Jewett will use to shape her narrative. As the winds continue to blow, Mrs. Todd says "half to herself: 'This makes me think o' the night Mis' Cap'n Tolland died. . . . Folks used to say these gales only blew when somebody's a-dyin', or the devil was a-comin' for his own, but the worst man I ever knew died on a real pretty mornin' in June'" (160). The narrator's response, "You have never told me any ghost stories," fails to distract Mrs. Todd from her worries. Without meaning to oblige her hostess, Mrs. Todd tells the story of Mis' Tolland and by so doing tells a story of both this world and the other.

5. Sarah Orne Jewett, "The Foreigner," in Jewett, *The Country of the Pointed Firs and Other Stories,* ed. Mary Ellen Chase (New York, 1981). Subsequent references are given parenthetically in the text.

Ironically, as its title story suggests, "The Foreigner" is about a woman whom an entire community regards as other. As Sarah Sherman argues, the sketch "does not celebrate community but reflects on its failure."[6] Mrs. Todd starts, stops, and begins again several times and eventually narrates the story of a woman whom the community regards as an outsider. Her difference from the other villagers is signaled by her origins—she was a French-born woman whom Cap'n Tolland met in Jamaica—her status as an artist—she plays the guitar and sings—and her effect on the community—it reproaches her for dancing. Mrs. Todd explains that her participation in this reproach did not cease until her mother, Mrs. Blackett, insisted that she visit Mis' Tolland. Even then, the foreigner had to win Mrs. Todd's sympathy and approval. She says, "When I see tears in her eyes 'twas all right between us" (170). It is only after Mis' Tolland dies that Mrs. Todd discovers that the foreigner had paid her the ultimate compliment of putting her in her will.

But just when the narrator assumes that this story of failed community and reluctant friendship has ended, Mrs. Todd re-enters her narrative to share what she had left out. She says, "I ain't told you all . . . no I haven't spoken of all to but very few" (182). The narrator observes that Mrs. Todd assumes her familiar countenance of an "old prophetess" or "sibyl" (183). She then solemnly and movingly recounts the story of Mis' Tolland's last night of life. As she sat at her bedside, she and Mis' Tolland witnessed the appearance of a shape, "a woman's dark face lookin' right at us" for "but an instant" (184). Mis' Tolland asks, "You saw her didn't you? . . . 'tis my mother." Mrs. Todd responds, *"Yes, dear I did; you ain't never goin' to feel strange an' lonesome no more."* She adds that "in a few quiet minutes 'twas all over. I felt they'd gone away together" (186).

In the last of the story's seven sections, Mrs. Todd ends her narrative with the words: "'Twas just such a night as this. I've

---

6. Sherman, *Sarah Orne Jewett*, 239.

told the circumstances to but very few; but I don't call it beyond reason. When folks is goin' 'tis all natural, and only common things can jar upon the mind. You know plain enough there's somethin' beyond this world; the doors stand wide open. 'There's somethin' of us that must live on; we've got to join both worlds together an' live in one but for the other.' The doctor said that to me one day" (187). This sketch reiterates the concepts I have attempted to examine about the cultural function of narrative in Jewett's fiction. First, by using the narrative framing device of a story-within-a-story, a storytelling event occasions another opportunity for the narrator to learn Dunnet Landing history. She not only learns more about this community's cultural roots, but she gets a new perspective on how its parochialism excludes the other and fails a woman who does not meet its standard of decorum. Moreover, the form of the story, with its multiple beginnings and endings, not only illustrates the mnemonic processes at work—that is, Mrs. Todd moving in and out of memory to construct the tale for her listener—but it illustrates both her desire and her reluctance to share so private a tale. As Deborah E. McDowell explains, "Narrative forces us to question our readings, to hold our judgment in check to continually revise it."[7] The stormy night thus occasions not only a new understanding and level of friendship between the narrator and Mrs. Todd, but it empowers Mrs. Todd to confront a difficult memory in her past. Both the teller and the listener are transformed in the telling of the tale. Moreover, because this narrative enables the reader to gain a new perspective on Mrs. Todd, on her relationship with the narrator, on the community of women and men at Dunnet Landing, and on that community's response to death and dying, it suggests how the consciousness of the reader might also be transformed. Like *Deephaven, The Country of the Pointed Firs,* and Jewett's various other sketches, "The Foreigner" allows Jewett

7. Deborah E. McDowell, "Boundaries: Distant Relations and Close Kin," in *Afro-American Literary Study in the 1990s,* ed. Houston A. Baker, Jr., and Patricia Redmond (Chicago, 1989), 68.

to engage in cultural critique and affirmation at one and the same time.

Toni Morrison's award-winning novel *Beloved* also extends our understanding of how the cultural function of narrative is inscribed in a woman's text. Based on an actual account of a slave mother who killed her child to prevent that child from being sold into slavery, it too focuses on themes of a community's response to the other, on death and dying, and on the role of memory in constructing our stories of the past. Like Mrs. Todd, Sethe has a difficult story to tell, and also like Mrs. Todd, she struggles with the telling, for it evokes a past she has tried to forget. In the words of the novel, she engages herself with the "serious work of beating back the past."[8] Whereas Jewett's sketch ends with a ghost story, Morrison's begins with one. The novel begins with the words "124 was spiteful" and thus both puts the reader off and invites her or him to read on. Morrison says this confrontational tone was purposeful: "Whatever the risks of confronting the reader with what must be immediately incomprehensible in that simple declarative authoritative sentence, the risk of unsettling him or her, I determined to take. . . . The reader is snatched, yanked, thrown into an environment completely foreign. . . . Snatched just as the slaves were from one place to another, from any place to another, without preparation and without defense."[9]

In personifying these numerals and the house they represent, Morrison introduces the reader to the ghost of the baby girl inhabiting Sethe's home along with her and her daughter Denver.

8. Toni Morrison, *Beloved* (New York, 1987), 73. Subsequent references are given parenthetically in the text. In *Beloved* Morrison extends the continuum of myth and folklore to memory and history. By doing so, she invites the reader to consider the cultural function of narrative for its ability to engender transformation and to heal the psychic wounds of slavery. I discuss this novel more extensively in my article "A Different Remembering: Memory, History, and Meaning in Toni Morrison's *Beloved*," in *Toni Morrison,* ed. Harold Bloom (New York, 1990), 189–99, and plan to treat it still more thoroughly in my next book, whose working title is "Spaces for the Reader: Toni Morrison's Narrative Poetics."

9. Morrison, "Unspeakable Things Unspoken," 32.

Her mother-in-law, Baby Suggs, has died and her sons have abandoned her, unable to stand the ghost or the community's rejection of their very different household. Sethe and her daughter Denver attempt to summon the ghost, hoping that "by calling forth the ghost" they could end the persecution with "a conversation . . . an exchange of views or something" (4). The process of trying to summon the ghost not only forces Sethe into the unwanted memory of having to trade sex for letters on her dead baby's gravestone but it also recalls the act of taking the child's life to save her.

As the novel progresses, Paul D, one of the men who had lived on the Sweet Home plantation with Sethe, arrives at 124, takes up with Sethe, and proceeds to drive out the angry, jealous ghost. The spirit of Sethe's lost baby then returns, reincarnated as the young woman Beloved. From then on, the novel is concerned primarily with this presence and its meaning for Sethe and Denver. Literally the presence of the past in the present, Beloved becomes the center of attention in the lives of both mother and daughter. For Sethe, whose pain and mourning over her murdered child recall Demeter's pain in losing Persephone to the underworld, Beloved's presence evokes an obsessive love. For Denver, Beloved becomes a cherished possession to be guarded greedily.

In one passage, the two share a dialogue that illustrates how narrative operates through history and memory in this novel. After swallowing "twice to prepare for the telling, to construct out of the strings she had heard all her life a net to hold Beloved" (76), Denver attempts to oblige her request to tell how she herself was born:

> Denver stopped and sighed. This was the part of the story she loved . . . she loved it because it was all about herself. . . . Now, watching Beloved's alert and hungry face, how she took in every word, asking questions about the color of things and their size, her downright craving to know, Denver began to see what she was

saying and not just to hear it. . . . Denver was seeing it now and
feeling it—through Beloved. Feeling how it must have felt to her
mother. . . . And the more detail she provided, the more Beloved
liked it. So she anticipated the questions by giving blood to scraps her
mother and grandmother had told her. (77–78)

The passage goes on to describe how Denver's monologue becomes a duet and "the two did the best they could to create what
really happened, how it really was" (78). The narrative thus becomes a collaborative telling of the story. As in Jewett's story, the
narrative framing device shapes this passage. Drawing on the history of the mother and grandmother, Denver tells a story that is
both rooted in the past and nurtured by her desire to connect with
the newest member of their household. Narrative becomes not
just a vehicle for sharing the story of Denver's life but what Peter
Brooks refers to as the metaphorical glue holding events and
memories together. Like Jewett's sketch, *Beloved* inscribes the
story of a mother-daughter reunion, of female bonding into a
community of women, and of the connection between this world
and the next.

More important, *Beloved* reminds us that narrative can transform both the listener and the teller. As Henry Louis Gates, Jr.,
asserts, "The stories we tell ourselves and our children function
to order our world, serving to create both a foundation upon
which each of us constructs our sense of reality and a filter
through which we process each event that confronts us every
day."[10] Through the matrix of myth and folklore Sarah Orne
Jewett and Toni Morrison tell the stories we have not heard, the
ones we need to hear and the ones we need to hear again. Narrative has the dual role, therefore, of being something told and of
being a way of knowing. It not only teaches us to value our ancestors but the value of *nommo*—the power of the word—to help

10. Henry Louis Gates, Jr., "Introduction: Narration and Cultural Memory in
the African-American Tradition," in *Talk That Talk: An Anthology of African
American Storytelling*, ed. Linda Goss and Marian E. Barnes (New York, 1989), 17.

us name ourselves and shape our lives in the tradition of our ancestors. As Morrison says of her own fiction, it is "both print and
oral literature."[11] Ultimately, these writers' use of the oral tradition evokes the same reciprocal relationship between teller and
listener as the African tradition of call and response and the Greek
tradition of choral commentary. On their individual literary journeys, both writers sought to create this reciprocal relationship between their fiction and their readers. In the tradition of feminist
readers, each writer hopes "that other women will recognize
themselves in her story and join in the struggle to transform culture."[12] The achievement of Sarah Orne Jewett and Toni Morrison
is that their folk aesthetic and mythic impulse affirm the value of
narrative for making such transformations possible. Telling the
stories of women across generations, their fiction not only offers
us roots to know our history but wings to pass it on.

11. Morrison, "Rootedness," 341.
12. Patrocinio P. Schweickart, "Reading Ourselves: Toward a Feminist Theory
of Reading," in *Speaking of Gender,* ed. Elaine Showalter (New York, 1989), 34.

BIBLIOGRAPHY

SARAH ORNE JEWETT

WORKS BY JEWETT
A Country Doctor. Boston, 1884.
The Country of the Pointed Firs and Other Stories. 1896. Reprint. Garden City, N.Y., 1956.
Deephaven and Other Stories. Edited by Richard Cary. New Haven, 1966.
"The Foreigner." In Sarah Orne Jewett, *The Country of the Pointed Firs and Other Stories,* edited by Mary Ellen Chase. New York, 1981.

WORKS ABOUT JEWETT
Afzal-Kahan, Fawzia. "Values and Vicissitudes of Ideology: The Feminist Genre of Sarah Orne Jewett's *Country of the Pointed Firs.*" Paper presented at the Sarah Orne Jewett Conference, Portland, Maine, June 17, 1985.
Ammons, Elizabeth. "Going in Circles: The Female Geography of Jewett's *Country of the Pointed Firs.*" *Studies in Literary Imagination,* XVI (Fall, 1983), 83–92.
———. "Jewett's Witches." In *Critical Essays on Sarah Orne Jewett,* edited by Gwen Nagel. Boston, 1984.
———. "The Shape of Violence in Jewett's 'A White Heron.'" *Colby Library Quarterly,* XXII (1986), 6–16.
Auchincloss, Louis. *Pioneers and Caretakers: A Study of Nine American Women Novelists.* Minneapolis, 1961.
Berthoff, Warner. "The Art of Jewett's *Pointed Firs.*" *New England Quarterly,* XXXII (March, 959), 31–53.
Bishop, Ferman. "The Sense of the Past in Sarah Orne Jewett." In *Appreciation of Sarah Orne Jewett: 29 Interpretive Essays,* edited by Richard Cary. Waterville, Maine, 1973.
Boggia-Sola, Jean. "The Poetic Realism of Sarah Orne Jewett." *Colby Library Quarterly,* VII (1965), 74–81.
Brenzo, Richard. "Free Heron or Dead Sparrow: Sylvia's Choice in Sarah Orne Jewett's 'A White Heron.'" *Colby Library Quarterly,* XIV (1978), 36–41.
Buchan, A. M. *Our Dear Sarah: An Essay on Sarah Orne Jewett.* St. Louis, 1942.
Cary, Richard. *Sarah Orne Jewett.* New York, 1962.
———, ed. *Appreciation of Sarah Orne Jewett: 29 Interpretive Essays.* Waterville, Maine, 1973.
———, ed. *Sarah Orne Jewett Letters.* Waterville, Maine, 1956.
Cather, Willa. *Not Under Forty.* New York, 1936.
Donovan, Josephine. *Sarah Orne Jewett.* New York, 1980.
———. "Sarah Orne Jewett's Critical Theory: Notes Toward a Feminine Literary Mode." In *Critical Essays on Sarah Orne Jewett,* edited by Gwen Nagel. Boston, 1984.
———. "A Woman's Vision of Transcendence: A New Interpretation of the Works of Sarah Orne Jewett." *Massachusetts Review,* XXI (1980), 365–80.

Eakin, Paul John. "Sarah Orne Jewett and the Meaning of Country Life." *American Literature*, XXXVIII (1967), 508–31.

Fagan, Susan Joan Martin. "Sarah Orne Jewett's Fiction: A Reevaluation from Three Perspectives." *Dissertation Abstracts International*, XLIII (August, 1982), 445A.

Fields, Annie, ed. *The Letters of Sarah Orne Jewett*. Boston, 1911.

Folsom, Marcia McClintock. "'Tact Is a Kind of Mind-Reading': Empathic Style in Sarah Orne Jewett's *The Country of the Pointed Firs*." In *Critical Essays on Sarah Orne Jewett*, edited by Gwen Nagel. Boston, 1984.

Frost, John Eldridge. *Sarah Orne Jewett*. Milford, N.H., 1960.

Horn, Robert L. "The Power of Jewett's *Deephaven*." *Colby Library Quarterly*, XI (1972), 617–43.

Hovet, Theodore R. "Once Upon a Time: Sarah Orne Jewett's 'A White Heron' as a Fairy Tale." *Studies in Short Fiction*, XV (1978), 63–68.

Howells, W. D. "Review of *Deephaven*." In *Critical Essays on Sarah Orne Jewett*, edited by Gwen Nagel. Boston, 1984.

Johns, Barbara. "'Mateless and Appealing': Growing into Spinsterhood in Sarah Orne Jewett." In *Critical Essays on Sarah Orne Jewett*, edited by Gwen Nagel. Boston, 1984.

Kraus, Mary C. "Sarah Orne Jewett and Temporal Continuity." *Colby Library Quarterly*, XV (1979), 157–74.

Leguin, Ursula K. "It Was a Dark and Stormy Night; or, Why Are We Huddling About the Campfire?" In *On Narrative*, edited by W. J. T. Mitchell. Chicago, 1980.

Matthiessen, Francis. *Sarah Orne Jewett*. Boston, 1929.

Mobley, Marilyn E. "Rituals of Flight and Return: The Ironic Journeys of Sarah Orne Jewett's Female Characters." *Colby Library Quarterly*, XXII (1986), 36–42.

Nagel, Gwen L., ed. *Sarah Orne Jewett: A Reference Guide*. Boston, 1978.

Nail, Rebecca Wall. "Where Every Prospect Pleases: Sarah Orne Jewett, South Berwick and the Importance of Place." In *Critical Essays on Sarah Orne Jewett*, edited by Gwen Nagel. Boston, 1984.

Noyes, Sylvia Gray. "Mrs. Almira Todd, Herbalist-Conjurer." *Colby Library Quarterly*, IX (1972), 643–49.

Pool, Eugene Hillhouse. "The Child in Sarah Orne Jewett." *Colby Library Quarterly*, VII (1967), 503–509.

Pry, Elmer. "Folk-Literary Aesthetics in *The Country of the Pointed Firs*." *Tennessee Folklore Society Bulletin*, XLIV (1978), 7–12.

Pryse, Marjorie. "Introduction to the Norton Edition." In Sarah Orne Jewett, *The Country of the Pointed Firs*. New York, 1981.

Renza, Louis A. *"A White Heron" and the Question of Minor Literature*. Madison, 1984.

Romines, Ann. "In Deephaven: Skirmishes Near the Swamp." *Colby Library Quarterly,* XVI (1980), 205–19.
Sherman, Sarah. *Sarah Orne Jewett: An American Persephone.* Hanover, N.H., 1989.
———. "Victorians and the Matriarchal Mythology: A Source for Mrs. Todd." *Colby Library Quarterly,* XXII (1986), 63–74.
Stevenson, Catherine Barnes. "The Double Consciousness of the Narrator in Sarah Orne Jewett's Fiction." *Colby Library Quarterly,* XI (1975), 1–12.
Thorp, Margaret Farrand. *Sarah Orne Jewett.* Minneapolis, 1966.
Westbrook, Perry D. *Acres of Flint: Sarah Orne Jewett and Her Contemporaries.* Rev. ed. Methuen, N.J., 1981.

TONI MORRISON

WORKS BY MORRISON
"Behind the Making of *The Black Book.*" *Black World,* XXIII (February, 1974), 86–90.
The Bluest Eye. New York, 1970.
"Cinderella's Stepsisters." In *Responding to Writing: A Reader for Writers,* edited by Judith Fishman. Indianapolis, 1983.
"City Limits, Village Values: Concepts of the Neighborhood in Black Fiction." In *Literature and the Urban Experience: Essays on the City and Literature,* edited by Michael C. Jaye and Ann Chalmer Watts. New Brunswick, 1981.
"Rootedness: The Ancestor as Foundation." In *Black Women Writers (1950–1980): A Critical Evaluation,* edited by Marie Evans. New York, 1984.
Song of Solomon. New York, 1977.
Sula. New York, 1973.
Tar Baby. New York, 1981.
"Unspeakable Things Unspoken: The Afro-American Presence in American Literature." *Michigan Quarterly Review,* XXVIII (Winter, 1989), 1–34.

WORKS ABOUT MORRISON
Albrecht, Brian E. "Toni Morrison: Lorain Writer No Slave to Success." Cleveland *Plain Dealer,* April 14, 1981, Sec. B, p. 5.
Bell, Pearl K. "Self-Seekers." *Commentary,* LXXII (August, 1981), 56–58.
Blake, Susan L. "Folklore and Community in *Song of Solomon.*" *MELUS,* VII (Fall, 1980), 77–82.
Brenner, Gerry. "*Song of Solomon:* Rejecting Rank's Monomyth and Feminism." In *Critical Essays on Toni Morrison,* edited by Nellie McKay. Boston, 1988.
Campbell, Josie P. "To Sing the Song, to Tell the Tale: A Study of Toni Morrison and Simone Schwarz-Bart." *Comparative Literature Studies,* XXII (Fall, 1985), 394–412.

Croyden, Margaret. "Toni Morrison Tries Her Hand at Playwriting." *New York Times,* December 29 1985, Sec. H, p. 6.

Davis, Cynthia A. "Self, Society, and Myth in Toni Morrison's Fiction." *Contemporary Literature,* XXIII (Summer, 1982), 323–42.

de Weever, Jacqueline. "Toni Morrison's Use of Fairy Tale, Folk Tale, and Myth in *Song of Solomon." Southern Folklore Quarterly,* XLIV (1980), 131–44.

Erickson, Peter B. "Images of Nurturance in Toni Morrison's *Tar Baby." CLA Journal,* XXVIII (1984), 11–32.

Harris, Leslie A. "Myth as Structure in Toni Morrison's *Song of Solomon." MELUS,* VII (1980), 69–82.

Hovet, Grace Ann, and Barbara Lounsberry. "Flying as Symbol and Legend in Toni Morrison's *The Bluest Eye, Sula,* and *Song of Solomon." CLA Journal,* XXVII (December, 1983), 119–40.

Le Clair, Thomas. "The Language Must Not Sweat: A Conversation with Toni Morrison." *New Republic,* March 2, 1981, pp. 25–29.

Lee, Dorothy H. "*Song of Solomon:* To Ride the Air." *Black American Literature Forum,* XVI (1982), 64–70.

McCluskey, Audrey. "A Conversation with Toni Morrison." In *Women in the Arts: A Celebration.* Bloomington, 1986.

McDowell, Edwin. "Behind the Best Sellers: Toni Morrison." *New York Times Book Review,* July 5, 1981, p. 18.

McKay, Nellie. "An Interview with Toni Morrison." *Contemporary Literature,* XXIV (Winter, 1983), 413–29.

Mobley, Marilyn E. "A Different Remembering: Memory, History, and Meaning in Toni Morrison's *Beloved."* In *Toni Morrison,* edited by Harold Bloom. New York, 1990.

——. "Narrative Dilemma: Jadine as Cultural Orphan in Toni Morrison's *Tar Baby,"* *Southern Review,* XXIII (October, 1987), 761–70.

Naylor, Gloria, and Toni Morrison. "A Conversation." *Southern Review,* XXI (1985), 567–93.

O'Shaughnessy, Kathleen. "'Life life life life': The Community as Chorus in *Song of Solomon."* In *Critical Essays on Toni Morrison,* edited by Nellie McKay. Boston, 1988.

Samuels, Wilfred D. "Liminality and the Search for Self in Toni Morrison's *Song of Solomon." Minority Voices* (1981), 59–68.

Skerrett, Joseph T., Jr. "Recitation to the Griot: Storytelling and Learning in Morrison's *Song of Solomon."* In *Conjuring: Black Women, Fiction, and Literary Tradition,* edited by Marjorie Pryse and Hortense J. Spillers. Bloomington, 1985.

Smith, Valerie. "The Quest for and Discovery of Identity in Toni Morrison's *Song of Solomon." Southern Review,* XXI (1985), 721–32.

Strouse, Jean. "Toni Morrison's Black Magic." *Newsweek,* March 30, 1981, pp. 52–57.

Wagner, Linda W. "Toni Morrison: Mastery of Narrative." In *Contemporary American Women Writers*, edited by Catherine Rainwater and William J. Scheick. Lexington, 1985.

Werner, Craig. "The Briar Patch as Modernist Myth: Morrison, Barthes, and Tar Baby as Is." In *Critical Essays on Toni Morrison*, edited by Nellie McKay. Boston, 1988.

Willis, Susan. "Eruptions of Funk: Historicizing Toni Morrison." In *Black American Literature and Literary Theory*, edited by Henry Louis Gates, Jr. New York, 1984.

OTHER WORKS CONSULTED

Abrahams, Roger, ed. *Afro-American Folktales: Stories from Black Traditions in the New World*. New York, 1985.

Adams, Henry. *The Education of Henry Adams*. New York, 1931.

Auerbach, Nina. *Communities of Women: An Idea in Fiction*. Cambridge, Mass., 1978.

———. *Woman and the Demon: The Life of a Victorian Myth*. Cambridge, 1982.

Awkward, Michael. *Inspiriting Influences: Tradition, Revision, and Afro-American Women's Novels*. New York, 1989.

Bachofen, Johann Jakob. *Myth, Religion, and Mother Right: Selected Writings of J. J. Bachofen*. Translated by Ralph Manheim. Princeton, 1967.

Bader, Julia. "The 'Rooted' Landscape and the Woman Writer." In *Teaching Women's Literature from a Regional Perspective*, edited by Lenore Hoffman and Deborah Rosenfelt. New York, 1982.

Bair, Barbara. "'Ties of Blood and Bonds of Fortune': The Cultural Construction of Gender in American Women's Fiction—An Interdisciplinary Analysis." Ph.D. dissertation, Brown University, 1984.

Baker, Houston A. *Blues, Ideology, and Afro-American Literature: A Vernacular Theory*. Chicago, 1984.

Bakhtin, Mikhail. "Form of Time and Chronotype in the Novel." In *The Dialogic Imagination: Four Essays by M. M. Bakhtin*. Edited by Michael Holquist. Translated by Caryl Emerson and Michael Holquist. Austin, 1981.

Baldwin, James. *Notes of a Native Son*. New York, 1964.

Barr, Marleen S., and Richard Feldstein, eds. *Discontented Discourses: Feminism, Textual Intervention, and Psychoanalysis*. Urbana, 1989.

Barthes, Roland. *Mythologies*. Translated by Annette Lavers. New York, 1972.

———. *S/Z*. Paris, 1970.

Bauer, Dale M. *Feminist Dialogics: A Theory of Failed Community*. Albany, 1988.

Baym, Nina. "Melodramas of Beset Manhood: How Theories of American Fiction Exclude Women Authors." *American Quarterly*, XXXIII (1981), 123–39.

Belenky, Mary Field, Blythe McVicker Clinchy, Nancy Rule Goldberger, and Jill Mattuck Tarule, eds. *Women's Ways of Knowing*. New York, 1986.

182

BIBLIOGRAPHY

Ben-Amos, Dan. "Toward a Definition of Folklore in Context." *Journal of American Folklore,* LXXXIV (1971), 3–15.
Benjamin, Jessica. *The Bonds of Love: Psychoanalysis, Feminism, and the Problem of Domination.* New York, 1988.
Benjamin, Walter. *Illuminations.* Edited by Hannah Arendt. New York, 1969.
Bernal, Martin. *The Fabrication of Ancient Greece, 1785–1985.* New Brunswick, 1987. Vol. I of Bernal, *Black Athena: The Afroasiatic Roots of Classical Civilization.*
Berthoff, Warner. *The Ferment of Realism: American Literature, 1884–1919.* New York, 1965.
Bettelheim, Bruno. *The Uses of Enchantment: The Meaning and Importance of Fairy Tales.* New York, 1976.
Bluefarb, Sam. *The Escape Motif in the American Novel: Mark Twain to Richard Wright.* Columbus, 1972.
Bluestein, Gene. *The Voice of the Folk: Folklore and American Literary Theory.* Amherst, 1972.
Brooks, Peter. *Reading for the Plot: Design and Intention in Narrative.* New York, 1984.
Bruck, Peter, and Wolfgang Karren, eds. *The Afro-American Novel Since 1960.* Amsterdam, 1982.
Bulkin, Elly. "An Interview with Adrienne Rich: Part II." *Conditions: Two,* October, 1977, pp. 53–66.
Bullfinch, Thomas. *Bullfinch's Mythology.* New York, 1978.
Byerman, Keith E. *Fingering the Jagged Grain: Tradition and Form in Recent Black Fiction.* Athens, Ga., 1985.
Cady, Edwin H. *The Road to Realism: The Early Years (1837–1885) of William Dean Howells.* Syracuse, 1956.
Campbell, Joseph. *The Hero with a Thousand Faces.* Princeton, 1949.
Carby, Hazel. *Reconstructing Womanhood: The Emergence of the Afro-American Woman Novelist.* New York, 1987.
Carter, Everett. *Howells and the Age of Realism.* Hamden, 1966.
Chase, Richard. *The Quest for Myth.* Baton Rouge, 1949.
Chatman, Seymour. "What Novels Can Do That Films Can't (and Vice Versa)." In *On Narrative,* edited by W. J. T. Mitchell. Chicago, 1980.
Christian, Barbara. *Black Feminist Criticism: Perspectives on Black Women Writers.* New York, 1985.
Cirlot, J. E. *A Dictionary of Symbols.* Translated by Jack Sage. London, 1977.
Donovan, Josephine. *Feminist Theory: The Intellectual Traditions of American Feminism.* New York, 1985.
———. *New England Local Color Literature: A Woman's Tradition.* New York, 1983.
Du Bois, W. E. B. *The Souls of Black Folk.* 1903, rpr. New York, 1968.

Dundes, Alan. *Interpreting Folklore*. Bloomington, 1980.

Eagleton, Terry. *Literary Theory*. Minneapolis, 1983.

Eliade, Mircea. *Myth and Reality*. New York, 1963.

———. *The Myth of the Eternal Return*. Princeton, 1954.

———. *Myths, Rites, Symbols: A Mircea Eliade Reader*. Edited by Wendell C. Beane and William G. Doty. 2 vols. New York, 1975.

Eliot, T. S. *Collected Poems, 1909–1962*. New York, 1963.

———. "Ulysses, Order, and Myth." *Dial*, LXXV (November 1923), 480–83.

Ellison, Ralph. *Shadow and Act*. New York, 1953.

Ellmann, Mary. *Thinking About Women*. New York, 1968.

Ellmann, Richard, and Charles Feidelson, Jr., eds., *The Modern Tradition*. New Haven, 1964.

Emerson, Ralph Waldo. *Selections from Ralph Waldo Emerson*. Edited by Stephen E. Whicher. Boston, 1957.

Evans, Marie, ed. *Black Woman Writers (1950–1980): A Critical Evaluation*. New York, 1984.

Fiedler, Leslie. *Love and Death in the American Novel*. Rev. ed. New York, 1966.

Fishel, Leslie H., and Benjamin Quarles, eds. *The Black American: A Documentary History*. Glenview, Ill., 1976.

Fisher, Dexter, ed. Minority Language and Literature: Retrospective and Perspective. New York, 1977.

Fisher, Dexter, and Robert B. Stepto, eds. *Afro-American Literature: The Reconstruction of Instruction*. New York, 1979.

Frazer, Sir James. *The Golden Bough*. New York, 1951.

Frye, Northrop. *Anatomy of Criticism: Four Essays*. Princeton, 1957.

Gates, Henry Louis, Jr. "Introduction: Narration and Cultural Memory in the African-American Tradition." In *Talk That Talk: An Anthology of African-American Storytelling,* edited by Linda Goss and Marian E. Barnes. New York, 1989.

———. *The Signifying Monkey: A Theory of Afro-American Literary Criticism*. New York, 1988.

———, ed. *Black Literature and Literary Theory*. New York, 1984.

Genette, Gerard. *Narrative Discourse: An Essay in Method*. Translated by Jane E. Lewin. Ithaca, 1980.

Georges, Robert A. "Toward an Understanding of Storytelling Events." *Journal of American Folklore,* XXVIII (1969), 313–28.

Georgia Writers Project. *Drums and Shadow*. Athens, Ga., 1940.

Graves, Robert. *Greek Myths*. Vols. I and II. New York, 1955.

Greene, Gayle, and Coppelia Kahn, eds. *Making a Difference: Feminist Literary Criticism*. London, 1985.

Grimms' Fairy Tales. New York, 1985.

Haley, Alex. *Roots: The Saga of an American Family.* Garden City, N.Y., 1976.

Harper, Michael S., and Robert B. Stepto, eds. *Chant of Saints.* Chicago, 1979.

Hassan, Ihab. *Radical Innocence: Studies in the Contemporary American Novel.* New York, 1961.

Hemenway, Robert. "Are You a Flying Lark or a Setting Dove?" In *Afro-American Literature: The Reconstruction of Instruction,* edited by Dexter Fisher and Robert B. Stepto. New York, 1979.

Henderson, Mae. "Speaking in Tongues: Dialogics, Dialectics, and the Black Woman Writer's Literary Tradition." In *Changing Our Own Words: Essays on Criticism, Theory, and Writing by Black Women,* edited by Cheryl A. Wall. New Brunswick, 1989.

Hillman, James. *Healing Fiction.* New York, 1983.

Hirsch, Marianne. *The Mother/Daughter Plot: Narrative, Psychoanalysis, Feminism.* Bloomington, 1989.

Hobbs, Glenda. "Harriet Arnow's Kentucky Novels: Beyond Local Color." In *Regionalism and the Female Imagination: A Collection of Essays,* edited by Emily Toth. New York, 1985.

Hoffman, Lenore, and Deborah Rosenfelt, eds. *Teaching Women's Literature from a Regional Perspective.* New York, 1982.

Hopkins, Bennett. *Important Dates in Afro-American History.* New York, 1969.

Iser, Wolfgang. *The Implied Reader: Patterns of Communication in Prose Fiction from Bunyan to Beckett.* Baltimore, 1974.

Jameson, Fredric. *The Political Unconscious: Narrative as a Socially Symbolic Act.* Ithaca, 1981.

JanMohamed, Abdul R. *Manichean Aesthetics: The Politics of Literature in Colonial Africa.* Amherst, 1983.

Jung, C. G. "The Psychological Function of Archetypes" and "The Principal Archetypes." In *The Modern Tradition,* edited by Richard Ellmann and Charles Feidelson, Jr. New Haven, 1964.

Kolodny, Annette. "A Map for Rereading; or, Gender and the Interpretation of Literary Texts." *New Literary History,* II (1980), 451–67.

Lévi-Strauss, Claude. *The Raw and the Cooked: Introduction to a Science of Mythology.* Translated by John Weightman and Doreen Weightman. New York, 1969.

Limon, José E. "Western Marxism and Folklore: A Critical Introduction." *Journal of American Folklore,* XCVI (1983), 34–52.

McDowell, Deborah E. "Boundaries; or, Distant Relations and Close Kin." In *Afro-American Literary Study in the 1990s,* edited by Houston A. Baker, Jr., and Patricia Redmond. Chicago, 1989.

Machann, Virginia Sue Brown. "American Perspectives on Women's Initiations: The Mythic and Realistic Coming to Consciousness." *Dissertation Abstracts International,* XL (1979), 1470A.

Martin, Jay. *Harvests of Change: American Literature, 1865–1914.* Englewood Cliffs, N.J., 1967.

Michie, Helena. "Not One of the Family: The Repression of the Other Woman in Feminist Theory." In *Discontented Discourses: Feminism, Textual Intervention, and Psychoanalysis,* edited by Marleen S. Barr and Richard Feldstein. Urbana, 1989.

Noble, Jeanne. *Beautiful Also Are the Souls of My Black Sisters.* Englewood Cliffs, N.J., 1978.

Padus, Emrika. *Woman's Encyclopedia of Health and Natural Healing.* Emmaus, Pa., 1981.

Patai, Raphael. *Myth and Modern Man.* Englewood Cliffs, N.J., 1972.

Pater, Walter. "The Myth of Demeter and Persephone." *Fortnightly Review,* January–February, 1876.

Pearson, Carol, and Katherine Pope. *The Female Hero in American and British Literature.* New York, 1981.

Pratt, Annis. *Archetypal Patterns in Women's Fiction.* Bloomington, 1981.

———. "Women and Nature in Modern Fiction." *Contemporary Literature,* XIII (1972), 476–90.

Propp, Vladimir. *Morphology of the Folktale.* Austin, 1968.

Pryse, Marjorie, and Hortense J. Spillers, eds. *Conjuring: Black Women, Fiction, and Literary Tradition.* Bloomington, 1985.

Rabuzzi, Kathryn Allen. *The Sacred and the Feminine: Toward a Theology of Housework.* New York, 1982.

Rainwater, Catherine, and William J. Scheick, eds. *Contemporary American Women Writers.* Lexington, Ky., 1985.

Ray, William. *Literary Meaning: From Phenomenology to Deconstruction.* Oxford, 1984.

Rich, Adrienne. *Of Woman Born: Motherhood as Experience and Institution.* New York, 1986.

———. "When We Dead Awaken: Writing as Re-Vision." *College English,* XXXIV (October, 1972), 18–26.

Ricoeur, Paul. "Narrative Time." In *On Narrative,* edited by W. J. T. Mitchell. Chicago, 1980.

Rimmon-Kenan, Shlomith. *Narrative Fiction: Contemporary Poetics.* New York, 1983.

Rourke, Constance. *The Roots of American Culture and Other Essays.* New York, 1942.

Ruas, Charles. *Conversations with American Writers.* New York, 1985.

Schafer, Roy. "Narrative in the Psychoanalytic Dialogue." In *On Narrative,* edited by W. J. T. Mitchell. Chicago, 1980.

Scholes, Robert, and Robert Kellogg. *The Nature of Narrative.* New York, 1966.

Schweickart, Patrocinio. "Reading Ourselves: Toward a Feminist Theory of Reading." In *Speaking of Gender,* edited by Elaine Showalter. New York, 1989.

Sheppard, R. Z. "Quiet Please, Writers Talking." Review of *Conversations with American Writers*, by Charles Ruas. *Time*, December 24, 1984, pp. 68–69.

Slochower, Harry. *Mythopoesis: Mythic Patterns in the Literary Classics*. Detroit, 1970.

Smith, Barbara H. "Narrative Versions, Narrative Theories." In *On Narrative*, edited by W. J. T. Mitchell. Chicago, 1980.

Spacks, Patricia Meyer. *The Female Imagination*. New York, 1975.

Spillers, Hortense. "Cross-Currents, Discontinuities: Black Women's Fiction." In *Conjuring: Black Women, Fiction, and Literary Tradition*, edited by Marjorie Pryse and Hortense Spillers. Bloomington, 1985.

Stepto, Robert B. and Michael S. Harper, eds. *Chant of Saints*, Chicago, 1979.

Suleiman, Susan R., and Inge Crosman, eds. *The Reader in the Text: Essays on Audience and Interpretation*. Princeton, 1980.

Synnestvedt, Sig. *The Essential Swedenborg: Basic Teachings of Emmanuel Swedenborg, Scientist, Philosopher, and Theologian*. New York, 1970.

Tate, Claudia, ed. *Black Women Writers at Work*. New York, 1983.

Thompkins, Jane P. *Reader-Response Criticism: From Formalism to Post-Structuralism*. Baltimore, 1980.

Thrall, William Flint, and Addison Hibbard. *A Handbook of Literature*. New York, 1960.

Toth, Emily, ed. *Regionalism and the Female Imagination*. New York, 1985.

Walker, Alice. *In Search of Our Mothers' Gardens*. New York, 1983.

Wall, Cheryl A. "Zora Neale Hurston: Changing Her Own Words." In *American Novelists Revisted: Essays in Feminist Criticism*, edited by Fritz Fleischmann. Boston, 1982.

———, ed. *Changing Our Own Words: Essays on Criticism, Theory, and Writing by Black Women*. New Brunswick, 1989.

Warhol, Robyn R. "Toward a Theory of the Engaging Narrator: Earnest Interventions in Gaskell, Stowe, Eliot." *PMLA*, CI (1986), 811–18.

Washington, Mary Helen. "An Approach to the Study of Black Women Writers." In *But Some of Us Are Brave*, edited by Gloria T. Hull *et al.* Old Westbury, 1982.

Westbrook, Perry D. *The New England Town in Fact and Fiction*. Madison, N.J., 1982.

White, Hayden. "The Value of Narrativity in the Representation of Reality." In *On Narrative*, edited by W. J. T. Mitchell. Chicago, 1980.

Whitman, Walt. *Complete Poetry and Selected Prose by Walt Whitman*. Edited by James E. Miller. Boston, 1959.

Willis, Susan. *Specifying: Black Women Writing the American Experience*. Madison, 1987.

Wood, Ann Douglas. "The Literature of Impoverishment: The Women Local Col-
orists in America, 1865–1914." *Women's Studies,* I (1972), 3–46.
Woodson, Carter G. *The Miseducation of the Negro.* Washington, D.C., 1903.
Woolf, Virginia. *A Room of One's Own.* New York, 1929.
Zagarell, Sandra A. "Narrative of Community: The Identification of a Genre."
Signs, XIII (Spring, 1988), 498–527.

INDEX

Morrison, 99, 109–17, 119–20; definition of, 168; gender differences in, 168–69
Sula. See Morrison, Toni
Swedenborg, Emanuel, 45, 52

Tar Baby. See Morrison, Toni
Tar baby folktale, 157–59, 162, 163, 167
Till, Emmett, 101, 101*n*19
Tiresias myth, 121
Trickster figure, 149, 149*n*23

Visitor motif, 30, 51–52

Walker, Alice, 3, 4, 26, 93, 143
Westbrook, Jay, 6*n*12
White, Hayden, 14
"A White Heron." *See* Jewett, Sarah Orne
Whitman, Walt, 3
Williams, John A., 7
Wood, Ann Douglas, 22, 61, 89
Woodson, Carter G., 152
Woolf, Virginia, 139

Yeats, W. B., 14

Zagarell, Sandra A., 129